WRITING WELL
for Work and Pleasure

THE NEW WRITER'S GUIDE TO
PRODUCING FEARLESS CONTENT

WRITING WELL
for Work and Pleasure

THE NEW WRITER'S GUIDE TO
PRODUCING FEARLESS CONTENT

Books, reports,
white papers, blogs,
articles etc.

ROBERT KELSEY

Writing Well for Work and Pleasure

© Robert Kelsey 2021

ISBN: 978-1-739841317 (paperback)

ISBN: 978-1-739841300 (ebook)

Published by John Wilkes Publishing under the imprint:

WILKES...

**Requests to publish work from this book
should be sent to the author.**

Photo by Florian Klauer on Unsplash

Printed and bound by CPI Group (UK) Ltd, Croydon CR0 4YY

Praise for Writing Well for Work and Pleasure

"This is a practical handbook for anyone who needs to write well, for either work or fun. If you follow Robert Kelsey's advice you will produce better prose, which will be both easier for readers to understand and more persuasive, whichever audience you are addressing. I strongly recommend it."

Luke Johnson, columnist, author, serial entrepreneur and Chairman of Risk Capital Partners

"This book will teach you not just how to write, but how to develop a robust point of view, how each sentence must live up to the promise of the last sentence and, crucially, how to intellectually engage with any subject that you choose to write about. Robert's training gave me tools that I still use every day: whether it is debating at home or at work, developing business plans, writing white papers or typing a simple email. A must read for anyone who wants to improve how they communicate through the written word."

Brian Buckley, Chief Marketing Officer at Nasdaq

"Training under Rob gave me the confidence to tell a story. Fresh out of university I had all the enthusiasm but none of skills to build a career in journalism. With his training and mentorship, I was given the tools to turn the complex financial story into something clear, concise and consumable. So happy the book he always spoke of writing is now a reality!"

Caroline Hyde, TV anchor and journalist at Bloomberg

"I thought I was a great writer until I worked for Rob. Time after time, he would throw back an article that was full of carefully-worded sentences and technical financial prose, which I had spent hours sourcing and composing. It would be covered in red ink and structure pyramids and a mass of various editorial signs indicating that it was just not up to scratch. I'd leave the office, deflated, with the messy papers stuffed into my bag. Until one day, finally, he handed a piece of work back to me with only a couple of marks on it. 'Not bad,' he shrugged. 'Getting there.' I wanted to frame it.

"Rob instilled in me a dedication to simplicity, clarity, diligence and the highest standards, underscored by an empathy for one's audience. These qualities have served as a basis for my career."

Rosanna Konarzewski, Chief Communications Officer at Millennium Investment Management

"I was fortunate to learn from this master at an early stage in my career and I still apply Rob's blueprint/teachings/methodologies daily some 20 years later. Whatever the purpose of your copy writing, this book will teach you how to bring your reader in and how to keep them reading until the end, indeed wanting more."

Fred Duff Gordon, Partner at Digitalis

"The techniques contained in this book liberated me into a 20-year career across all types of media writing — including journalism, fiction, and communications. I would recommend it to anyone seeking to start or refresh a career based on the written word."

Toby Guise, writer and media consultant

Table of Contents

Preface

What's the point of a preface I ask in Chapter Six? Why keep readers away from the main text of your writing project with so much preamble and bombast? Forewords and introductions, biographies, acknowledgements and dedications as well as prefaces to various editions. On and on it goes with the reader growing ever more impatient to get to the start of the book: to Chapter One, page one, line one.

Two reasons justify a preface in my view. The reader needs to know something about their journey through the pages ahead. Perhaps a warning about the terrain: bendy and smooth in equal measure though with a fantastic view from the top. It could be a mood or sense-check — informing the reader of what to expect while adding a warning regarding the tone or attitude as well as what they will and won't find within.

Second, the writer might need to explain why they've written it. Their author journey. What compelled them to write and why they're singularly qualified to do so. In part, this can come from the author's insecurities — their need to offer justification.

Start with the sense check. Writing snobs or grammatical pedants will find this book irritating. It's not for them, though — when helpful — it mines the output of some of the best-known style and grammar guides (and there's a review of some of the most influential in the Appendix). The point of this book is to help people that have something to say or a desire to be heard and yet fear the writing challenge or feel their writing skills are inadequate.

Professionals, academics, students, analysts, amateur historians, hobbyists or wannabe polemicists: all are my target readership. Doctrinaire highbrow literary types, less so.

The joy of good writing is that it improves our communication skills across the piece, even verbally — a fantastic boon for the under-confident when presenting or for those who feel insecure or under-educated when dealing with language.

The pain is that this is the land of conceited pretension — of people all-too-willing to use language as a protective exclusionary barrier. Mocking as a form of gatekeeping. But they're usually insecure about their place within the inner sanctum so can be ignored. This book aims to kick down those gates using the very weapons they employ against us.

Self-justification

What about my author journey? My self-justification for writing this book? No doors were opened by my education, though plenty by my guile, which a 1970s Essex comprehensive education delivers by the bucketload. And while I can point to no biological hurdles — being pale, male and increasingly stale — my educational background jarred with the privilege around me, whether on the respected national newspaper where I started as a cub-journalist or the financial publisher where I progressed as an editor.

I blagged my way into both roles, as well as into a leading investment bank when I tired of journalism. But in all cases I had to learn how to survive, which meant learning skills others felt beneath them: such as page and production editing, sub-editing copy and in producing the unglamorous workaday content — as well as being better at the writing jobs coveted by others.

Even while a banker — now required to converse professionally with highly critical and often pompous internal and external audiences

— it was writing that helped me stay ahead of the class-based prejudices I faced in certain quarters.

Their enmity was a gnawing, cumulative, confidence-sapping drag on my advancement. Yet good writing undermined their derision of my accent or manners. They struggled to respond in kind, so that became how I expressed myself: in writing and by so powerfully honing my points they couldn't be ignored.

I was using prose as a pistol. And it became a weapon I developed for others via the public relations agency I founded after tiring of banking. The agency was focused on the very notion of "communicating expertise" (which became our strapline) — helping professionals overcome barriers to advancement by improving their communication skills, usually through creating great "content" (as the PR industry insists on calling the books, white papers, articles, blogs and more that we churn out on a daily basis on behalf of our clients).

I also started writing books, mostly on helping others navigate their mental barriers to achievement. Five books later; scores of white papers later (mostly ghost-written for our clients, many of whom have English as a second language); countless ghost-written articles later (as well as commentaries, features, interviews, Q&As, newsletters, awards submissions, proposals, blogs etc.) and I developed a *PowerPoint* lecture for our trainees. It was called *How to Write the Killer Commentary Article* and it forms the genesis of this book.

Yes, this book's focus is mainly on long-form projects such as books or white papers (which can take several formats, as explained within). But it also aids shorter-form writing tasks such as articles, commentaries, blogs, newsletters, websites etc. The processing, structuring and styling advice ahead will help, no matter what the format — or length — of your project, though the framework of the text is dominated, quite rightly, by the most ambitious of those projects: the book and (to a lesser extent) the white paper.

I hope this guide helps bring out the writer within. And I hope that doing so gives you as much inner confidence as writing has given me.

Robert Kelsey, London, 2021

PS. While I reject the need for acknowledgements (see Chapter Six), Finn Partners (who bought my PR firm Moorgate Communications) deserve special mention for their patience in dealing with me since the sale in 2019, especially the European head Chantal Bowman-Boyles, as well as the owner Peter Finn and the Financial Services teams in London, Frankfurt and New York. Thank you!

Chapter One

What to write and for whom

1. Why write?

"Everyone has a book in them." So goes the adage, to which literary wits (the late Christopher Hitchens among them) have added the caveat that "in most cases that's where it should stay".

Harsh but fair? Not at all. What's meant by the "book in them" aphorism is that everyone has something to say. Professionals in particular have a career's worth of wisdom to impart. Others a lifetime of experiences "on the frontline" that need recording for posterity. Young professionals will want to impress in order to climb the career ladder while idealists will want to be heard. Teachers need to inspire; artisans to explain their craft.

It might not be a book, of course. For ambitious professionals a white paper is the likely preference. Others may be asked to produce a report or be invited to contribute an article for a publication or website or even just a blogpost — all of which takes us rapidly to the point Hitchens & Co are making. That while everyone has a story to tell or some expertise to communicate, only a minority will have the writing skills required to do so, which is what every word of this book is dedicated to changing.

Writing is a craft. It can be taught and learnt. It's not a talent. Those wags chuckling in self-satisfaction as they shoot down the ambitions of would-be writers know this, and also know their craft was honed from their privilege — usually via an expensive Anglosphere education.

No, that's not me being "chippy". It's me telling-off the privileged for not recognising the advantages they gained from learning that craft early. So early, they sometimes mistake it for talent.

Having learnt their craft so young they've lost their fear of writing, it comes as naturally to them as a circus-child riding a horse or the trapeze. Yet it's still nurture. Still taught and learnt, just from an early age. So while we might learn it too late to acquire their assumption of innate talent, we can learn it nonetheless.

As an adult we'll also understand the context of what's being taught, making it a more exciting learning experience. And we can apply what we learn immediately. After all, anyone reading this book will likely have at least a vague notion of the writing project ahead of them. The one that terrified them enough to look for help.

Lose the fear

Writing well matters. It matters a lot. Heard of Charles Darwin? Of course you have. But what about his rival Alfred Russel Wallace? Me neither. In fact, he's almost entirely unheard of because, while both men were racing to claim evolutionary theory as their own — in fact initially collaborating — Darwin published *On the Origin of Species* in 1858, which grabbed the public's attention and made him the most celebrated naturalist of his age. Thereafter, Wallace — who outlived Darwin — was reduced to writing follow-up books with the word "Darwinism" in the title.

So be Darwin. Fearlessly claim the ground. And that means converting knowledge into words. Unrecorded experiences go unnoticed.

Sure, there are other media you could use, especially in our digital age. But even they require storyboards, scripts and "treatments" if they're to rise above the dross.

No matter what the format, good writing matters. Leaden prose, poor syntax, content burdened by hyperbole or over-accentuated adjectives: all undermine those with something to say. Yet there are books aplenty on style and punctuation, many cited in the pages ahead. This book dives into those details only so far as they matter for lifting our writing to the next level — helping us lose the fear of writing and allowing us to produce our best work.

Mostly, this book covers the process of writing, as well as the critical impact that process has on quality. If our goal is the imparting of knowledge via the written word — and doing so brilliantly — then the quality of our prose is but one part. In fact the last part, after first developing an argument, focusing on what to include, structuring it correctly and then — and only then — writing it compellingly.

Yes, it's hard work. Absolutely, it takes time and effort. But it's a step-by-step process — with each step leading to the next and with every step forward helping us banish our fear of the project underway.

2.   What to write

Let's start with format. While important for how we approach the task, the format can change. I've written many articles that have morphed into white papers, as well as the reverse. As for books: many start life in an entirely different form. My last book was triggered by an article for a magazine while my first book started life as an email to a friend. And, as stated, this book began life as a *PowerPoint* presentation for trainees.

Most would-be writers are attracted by the idea of a book, although probably the most common written output for professionals is a report or white paper. And then there are articles, usually in the form of commentary-style opinion pieces offered to specialist publications, often thanks to lobbying by public relations (PR) firms such as mine. Such articles are an increasing part of the job-spec for professionals, as are inhouse blogs. Again, it's often PR or marketing departments that are pushing sometimes reluctant executives — both senior and junior — for contributions.

And while there are obvious differences in length and style, there's significant crossover with respect to the process and execution, as well as in the editing — all of which this book covers in detail.

But let's first look at the differences.

a.   The book

These range in length from around 50,000 words to anything above 100,000. Most book page-designs average 300 words per page, and with the average book coming in at 250 pages that's 75,000 words. This sounds like a lot but, by the end of most writing projects, the problem is editing down the word length rather than the opposite (see Chapter Six).

Nonetheless, the theme of the book will need to justify such a commitment from both the writer and, just as importantly, the reader. Sketching a table of contents can help decide whether a book-length project is justifiable. Are there, say, ten chapters capable of 25 pages or 7500 words of text (note that Chapter One of this book is around 7000 words)?

Looked at another way: are there four distinct parts of roughly 15-20,000 words each? Certainly, that's how I approached my best-selling self-help book *What's Stopping You?* which dealt with four core topics: diagnosing the problem; imploring the reader to act; helping them develop a plan of action; and helping them deal with the barriers they'll face on their journey. Enthusiasm (and a little vanity) led me to add an unnecessary fifth (on entrepreneurship), but those four core elements justified the book.

b. Short books or pamphlets

The trend for self-publishing via processes such as *Amazon Kindle Direct Publishing* has somewhat liberated the book format. No longer the tyranny of the bookstore buyer expecting a standard product for their standard shelves. And this has triggered a renaissance in the short book.

Once known as pamphlets, short books can be as brief as 7000 words, with anything up to 30,000 (or 100 pages) still qualifying under this description. Historically, such pamphlets were the mainstay of the polemicist — usually writing feverishly on the political dilemma of the day (making speed an acute need). Martin Luther's *95 Theses* — nailed to a church door in Wittenberg, Germany, in 1517 — is probably the most famous (and influential) pamphlet in history. An early and devastating use of the printing press to stir opinions.

Other game-changing pamphlets include John Milton's 30-page *Areopagitica*, which defended free speech during the English Civil War; Thomas Paine's 50-page *Common Sense*, which inspired the American Revolution in 1776; and Émile Zola's 4000-word 1898 anti-establishment *J'Accuse...!* which blew open the Dreyfus affair in France. Martin Luther King Junior's 1963 *Letter from Birmingham Jail* shamed the US establishment into action in about 7000 words while George Orwell's 63-page 1941 *The Lion & The Unicorn* was an early treatise on the shape of post-war Britain.

All these famous examples are noteworthy for two further reasons. First, unlike full-length books they follow no strict format: ranging from an expanded list (Luther) to a written-up speech (Milton), a letter (Luther-King Jr) and a three-part mini-book (Orwell). Second, they transformed the influence of their authors — launching them into notoriety.

If you've something important to say — and it can't wait — a short book might just be your format.

c. White papers

The dictionary describes a white paper as "an authoritative report issued by any organisation" so my use of the term in this book encompasses just that: any document released by anyone with the purpose of being authoritative. This includes academic papers, even though these are often written for official journals, of which *The Lancet* is probably the most famous in the UK (in fact a family of journals covering all-things health-related).

Academic journals have their own rules, although they align with white papers in one key respect: they're about communicating the author's — or authors' given that many are co-written — expertise to an audience. And that differentiates white papers from reports that are no more than a factual account of something in particular, and potentially for the benefit of a single reader (perhaps the head of an organisation). That said, they still need to be well written.

Are white papers simply short books for professionals? Length-wise, tend to be at least 3000 words and up to around 10,000, so they broadly fit in that respect. They're often proposing significant changes in their field, so also align with the campaigning traditions of pamphleteering. In government circles they're the start of the legislative process, so form an official role and consequently follow their own rules on length, format and style. Meanwhile, in business, white papers have largely replaced product brochures, which — while being feel-good and glossy "leave-behinds" — are rarely read.

White papers tend to reverse the focus of a brochure, being less about a product offering and more about the concerns and needs of their intended audience. They are consequently more read (or downloaded) than their brochure equivalents. The sell is implicit rather than explicit, with the white paper propagating the author's understanding of — even empathy with — the target reader: all of which makes white papers a worthy inclusion within the bailiwick of this book.

They can certainly be glossy and these days tend to project high production values, including images and infographics and a beautiful page design and cover. Yet I'd defend the role of a document that spurns production values for immediacy: the "hot off the press" photocopied report that can change fortunes in an instant (Jerry Maguire's mission statement in the eponymous 1996 movie being a classic example).

Across the entire services sector, white papers have become a great way for professionals to raise their profile. And as PR tools, they're unbeatable. Consequently, I've ghost-written or edited scores of white papers for our PR clients, including some the world's largest and most prestigious financial institutions.

For those thinking they want to write something that communicates their knowledge and/or puts forward a particular viewpoint — especially within a professional context — white papers might well be the answer.

d.   Commentary articles

Or is it simply an article? For our purposes, I mean "thought leader-ship" or commentary pieces in which a point of view is expressed and attributed to a named individual. Sure, features, interviews and other works of pure journalism count, and their execution will benefit from this book. But the core writing output that concerns us here will be the "opinion piece" the "byline" the "commentary article" or the "OpEd" (meaning opposite the editorial page carrying the newspaper's view).

These are different names for essentially the same thing: an ex-pressed viewpoint of an expert or opinion-former (an "influencer" in PR-speak), usually on a single theme. They tend to be between 800 and 1200 words (1500 words max) — with anything above that creeping into the academic journal space and structured more as white papers. Here we mean something short and snappy.

Many will be peer-to-peer (or P2P) professional pieces, though commentary articles can be on anything: hobbies, pets, holidays, food, history, politics, health, astrology, celebrity-gossip — anything.

The byline is critical. This is you, the writer, with something to say. An opinion. Again, some are co-written with others, although this usually detracts from their power, which is the sharp punch of a lone expert — saying what's got to be said.

Which brings us to a potential hierarchy for the opinion-expressing formats described above. The book is at the top: the wise, languid aristocrat of the genre; and the commentary article at the bottom — the darting, furtive Artful Dodger. Which makes the white paper the middle-ranking professional: the ambitious *arriviste*, keen on being noticed.

Yet, as the pages ahead hopefully demonstrate, they're all trying to achieve the same thing — the relaying of knowledge and/or an opinion to an audience in narrative form. This means there are major overlaps with respect to process, content, structuring and style, making what's ahead relevant no matter what the intended output.

e. Blogs

These days, of course, there's a lower rung in the writing-format pecking order: blogs. These can be either for our own regular blog or as a guest blogger elsewhere, or — most commonly — as an article for a social media feed such as *LinkedIn* or *Facebook*.

By their very nature, blogs can be any length and obey no rules on style or format. Yet the best bloggers restrict their posts to below 1000 words (often as few as 500) — following the good blogger's "little and often" maxim. Regularity matters when trying to build an audience via a blog and short posts help retain the attention of fickle and easily distracted followers, who'll nonetheless come back regularly looking for more.

Yet this is the lowest rung in the pecking order for a reason. Blogs are too often shoddily written, poorly argued, wacky, self-indulgent writing diatribes. The format's very unedited liberation has given it a shambolic air. While readers approach a newspaper column expecting a well-structured, strongly reasoned argument (and may be disappointed), they tend to approach a blog with low or no expectations (and are hopefully pleasantly surprised).

Blogs should be engaging. They're indeed unedited, making the voice authentic. This allows for a deeper candour than the insider platitudes of more constricted formats (a problem tackled below). And this should encourage a loyal following that can be built over time, making blogs truly meritocratic.

And blogging opens up our world, particularly if we're an expert in a niche area — perhaps so niche we couldn't hope to win favour from a mainstream publication. A regular blog could be the answer: one discussing developments and experiences as well as swapping views with peers. No matter how narrow your field, there's either a blog covering it (to which you can contribute) or a fantastic opening to start one.

f.   Promotional material

Finally comes promotional material. This includes the product brochure as well as website copy, pitches and proposals (even if on *PowerPoint*) and even the lowly cold introductory letter or job application. Few people will go through life without having to write something that sells something — including themselves — so we might as well learn to write it well.

Promotional content mostly follows similar structures to the weightier formats above, or should do. And all those lessons to come — regarding considering angles, researching and curating content, structuring and presentation, and style — matter here too.

In fact, they matter more. As I tell our junior writers (often desperate to move off the "promotional content" beat), most people would rather be reading about Manchester United or Gwyneth Paltrow — or more likely watching videos on their iPhones. Grabbing and keeping their attention will be difficult, which makes their job the one needing the greatest writing skills. It's also the most important because livelihoods are at stake.

So make it compelling.

g.   Other media

Whatever you decide to write, write it. Don't waste your words on verbal or digital alternatives. If you say it rather than write it — perhaps at an industry event reading from a *PowerPoint* — your words are spent the second they leave your mouth. With no published record, your words are as good as lost. And they no longer belong to you, allowing others to utilise them without attribution. Only through publishing — in a written format — can you claim the idea as yours (though there is *SlideShare* for uploading presentations).

And while videos and podcasts feel both more immediate and more accessible, they're also more ephemeral. Digital formats come and go while the written word lasts.

As for podcasts: I've been involved in plenty — both to promote my books and to help clients get noticed. They're great, but all are now lost somewhere out there in the deep space of the internet, some of which I'm hoping no one will ever find. Yet my books and even articles are still there on Amazon (and other sites). Findable, buyable and readable. That's the power of the written word.

If in doubt, transport yourself back to the year 2000: placing, on your imaginary millennial table a DVD (a newish format, even then), a CD and a book. Now predict which one of the three will be the only publishing format to survive — and indeed thrive — into the 2020s. Yes, it's the only format that was also dominant in the 1920s, and the 1820s.

And a last point on recorded rather than written media: they too require writing skills, as well as an understanding of the content-generation process. They too need a focus on the audience, the angle and the content. They too need a structure and an appropriate style. Learn to write well, and you'll make better videos and podcasts. And you'll certainly write better *PowerPoints*.

3.   Your audience

Writing well is a skill you'll take to your grave. Acquiring that skill requires practice, diligence and discipline (see Chapter Two). But it's worth it. People that write well get to express themselves. They're listened to, and often it's their views that gain sway.

Yet the best writers are not the most correct writers. Sure, silly mistakes — in grammar, punctuation and word usage — will jar and eventually irritate the reader. But the beauty of English is that it's remarkably forgiving as a medium. It's a practical language. A highly adaptable hybrid. We're lucky in our native (or for some readers, chosen) tongue, though much of what lies ahead works in any language.

No, the best writers write for their audience. Not to show off or prove a point but to address the needs of their readers. To intrigue them, to persuade or inform them. When considering a writing project, the first consideration is therefore for whom do we write? If our finished work is no more than the downloading of our expertise or our (potentially highly prejudicial) views, it will have failed. Successful books, white papers or articles focus on the audience.

This impacts every element of our planned writing project and underpins the entire process. Our angle: if we write about an innovation it's that innovation's impact on our audience that matters, not just the technicalities. Our content: we'll need different supporting evidence and arguments for different audiences. Our structure: more conservative or official audiences will insist on facts and figures being presented in a particular way that won't suit others who'll perhaps want a more persuasive or emotive narrative. And our style: authoritative or engaging, official or conversational — though always compelling and with brevity whether writing for our betters, our peers or our neighbours.

Some target audiences below.

a.   Peer professionals

Almost exclusively, white papers focus on this group as will most articles in trade papers and professional journals. Our writing "voice" (see Chapter Five) needs to be credible while engaging: authoritative and evidenced while interesting and succinct. Brevity matters, yet the body copy needs to flow — to stand alone as understandable text without being reliant on constant cross-referencing and footnotes.

And while this is partially solved by addressing the audience — with the narrative coming first, overriding the need to offload facts — it means we have to navigate the choppy waters of assumed knowledge. Assume your reader has no knowledge of the subject and they could feel patronised, even insulted. Assume their knowledge is too deep, and your content will fly over their heads, leaving them confused, lost and looking for something more interesting to occupy them.

There's no easy answer, so I defer — as with so many other elements of writing — to *The Economist*. This is a weekly magazine aimed at intelligently covering a broad range of topics globally. And it seems to get it broadly right with respect to their readers' assumed knowledge. Its approach is best explained by an (invented) example: a sentence that includes references to, say, the current UK prime minister Boris Johnson, a major UK manufacturer (British Aerospace), and concepts such as defence procurement and government.

The Economist will assume the reader needs no explanation of widely understood concepts such as government and the role of the prime minister, while all people and organisations require a first-use introduction, as would non-universal concepts.

The resulting passage could read something like:

"An enquiry into Ministry of Defence spending with British Aerospace (BAe), a major arms manufacturer, has given UK prime minister Boris Johnson a problem with respect to defence procurement for the armed forces."

The Ministry of Defence escapes introduction because of its generic title (thus avoiding the unnecessary phrase "the Ministry of Defence, the UK defence ministry"). And the sentence also avoids an explicit explanation of defence procurement because the entire sentence is an account of the concept, making the explanation implicit. People and organisations, meanwhile, are introduced, no matter how well-known.

The aim is to broaden access for casual readers without talking down to the specialist, despite their almost certain pre-knowledge of the people, entities and concepts involved. Though please note: there's no universal answer to this conundrum. Writers have to calculate the assumed knowledge for every sentence they write, based on both their immediate and broader audiences.

b.   The wider public

Assumed knowledge matters here too, of course. Yet the key need when writing for the wider public is to entertain them. You might be trying to persuade them of your viewpoint or sell them your wares. But persuasion comes easier to those whose prose grips both the attention and the imagination of their readers.

The casual non-committed reader expects to be emotionally engaged, and they'll want you to deliver on your promises. A book advertised as fun will need to be fun. The same with trauma and sentimentality. They'll expect to ride the waves. Be gripped.

This doesn't mean being overly florid. Writing full of adjectives and adverbs will quickly lose its impact. But nor does it mean weighing down the text with overly long sentences burdened with sub-clauses and technicalities. It means adopting a style that suits the mood — with a pace and density to match.

It also means making it visual. Novels succeed because their entire premise relies upon visual imagery being triggered in the reader's mind. Non-fiction writing should do the same, especially for the casual reader. It's why case studies and anecdotes work. They convert the conceptual into the actual, allowing the reader a firmer grip on the visual imagery required for understanding.

And the best way to write visually is to think visually. For instance, in Chapter Four, I compare writing an article to building a skyscraper, with a concrete lift/elevator-shaft and sections manufactured separately and bolted together. Is that the only way to describe writing? Not at all. But as a visual reminder of the process it's fun, it's memorable and it works (that's a *tricolon*, by the way, see Chapter Five).

Writing for the wider public is also a good moment to introduce the "reader snag": trip-hazards within the text that temporarily flummox readers — leading, too often, to the loss of their attention and their capitulation soon after.

As part of the editing process, reader snags should be spotted and removed. Or save yourself some time and avoid adding them in the first place. How to find them? Try noticing when reading content produced by others: what hooks you in and keeps you reading; and what makes your attention wander or confuses you to the point it needs rereading?

Chances are, it's a reader snag: a word you've never previously encountered (most likely revealing the writer's vanity); a leaden or clumsy phrase; some strangulated syntax or a convoluted description; or maybe an off-point or diversion. Take note every time it happens.

c. The "great and the good"

No, I'm not going to say "break all the rules to get yourself noticed". That's just in the movies. Normally, the "great and the good" — i.e. the leaders in any professional set-up — are not looking for rule-breakers (just ask Jerry Maguire). At least not rule-breakers that haven't first served their apprenticeship, showing due deference to those in charge.

Certainly, "The Establishment" in any circle is a tough nut to crack. We live in a technocracy and here are Plato's guardians — the technocrats with a watchful eye on the entrance to their sanctum. And there's usually only one way in: to, indeed, get yourself noticed but in the right way. As an insider.

While that often means using academic and professional journals as your route to publication — at least initially — it doesn't prevent you publishing content elsewhere, either as a white paper or as rewritten versions for trade papers. We call this process "slice-and-dice" in our PR firm, in which we regenerate content for different audiences. It all helps clients "get noticed" even if it's the official journals that retain the most clout.

With this audience, it's critical to not undermine the all-important commodity of credibility. Everything has to be justified, making this the one audience where the "inverted pyramid" might not apply, or not apply fully. The inverted pyramid is a key concept for writing compelling non-fiction. It's explained fully in Chapter Four, though is — in essence — an inversion of the standard school essay in which *in-*

troduction, main-argument, conclusion is flipped to become *conclusion, justification, context* or maybe *conclusion, justification, consequences*.

That said, nothing's stopping you grabbing your audience's attention with your strongest claims stated upfront, although — if you're not to raise their defences — you'll quickly need to calm nerves with some qualifying context regarding your reasoning.

And their view of your opinion will be deeply coloured by their view of your journey in formulating that view. Otherwise, the cognitive dissonance (i.e. mental discomfort) you've induced in your opening — great for grabbing the attention of other audiences — could backfire.

d. Adversaries

Hmmm, how to write for those we oppose? This brings up one of the most important aspects of writing: the need to be read. If you simply want to express yourself in words, try poetry. This book is about using the written word to develop and communicate a point of view to new and wider audiences. It's for those with something to say but also with the desire to be heard. To persuade. And here we're facing our least generous audience, making self-indulgent writing wasteful in the extreme.

Unfortunately, we're also least attuned to this audience, which makes the temptation to lecture and hector — and even to insult — potentially overwhelming. But, as I often say to those I hear debating politics, you won't win people over by insulting them. The appalled looks I receive after saying this usually tell me that this was exactly what they were doing, and they'd either failed to consider this or simply didn't care.

As writers, our role is to persuade, so we should write with that in mind. A strong first exercise is therefore to seek alignment where we can. To start with and stress the commonalities. Some of the most successful politicians in recent decades have done exactly that: winning by empathising with their natural antagonists. Think of the Reagan Democrats or Bill Clinton's "triangulation" or the entire premise of Tony Blair's New Labour. All three were noted for winning debates, not by combat but through, first, demonstrating their empathetic understanding of how their natural opponents thought, which encouraged those opponents to at least listen.

And with the door open we must remain aware that it can snap shut, meaning we must build our case carefully. Step by small step, we should build upon rather than challenge the platform erected by our initial understanding and empathy. Of course, some arguments will jar: that's why they're our opponents — making the management-appraisal technique of the "shit sandwich" a useful potential concept. This starts with the positives (in this case areas of agreement) before shifting — respectfully and with empathy — towards the areas of contention, and then finishing on a harmonious note: perhaps a shared view of a better future.

Of course, there are times when it's just too tempting to lay out arguments as a series of certainties — bang, bang, bang — in an attempt to carpet-bomb your dimwit opponents into submission. This is a deliberate attempt at generating a state of cognitive dissonance, in which we first disabuse our adversaries of their fundamental beliefs before offering to rescue them via the positives of our view.

Certainly, I've done this myself on occasion, usually out of frustration. But I've always been surprised at how rarely such a full-frontal approach works. Positions become entrenched rather than undermined, that's if they even bother to continue engaging — making the carpet-bombing approach useful only for reinforcing (well-entrenched) allies rather than winning over potential recruits.

Two further points to consider when writing for adversaries. First, present a new angle rather than the same old tropes. Come at it from a different direction so that you're adding something refreshing. Second, focus on policies and outcomes rather than personal *ad hominem* attacks, which tend to make writers look embittered and petty, not least because they're almost certainly opining from second- or third-hand sources.

e.   Children and students

Attention is the problem here. Most non-fiction writing for children and students is educational and, as any teacher can tell you, once attention is lost, it's lost. Bringing the reader with you, while always important, is therefore critical when writing for the young and those in education.

And this can lead to some counter-intuitive recommendations. For instance, repetition — far from being anathema to good writing — is helpful. This doesn't mean pure repetition: saying a phrase over and over until it can be repeated on demand. It means ensuring that a concept, once explained, sticks.

One way of doing this is to repeat the central theme for each element. A history book, for example, could start paragraphs with: "Industrialisation's most important consequence was..." followed by "Yet industrialisation also led to..." and "Additionally, industrialisation generated..." and "Less obviously, industrialisation caused...".

Constantly, we're reminded that we're learning about the consequences of industrialisation. Each paragraph is part of a mental list being built by our narrative, with the relevance of each element obvious. We're only repeating the core descriptor (in this case "industrialisation"), which — while showing admirable brevity — might require periodic reinforcement using alternative descriptors such as "the factory system" or "new manufacturing processes".

Visualisation is another technique for bringing writing alive for the young and potentially reluctant. So those factories are noisy with thumping machinery, and the towns cramped and squalid or smelly. These aren't adjectives for the sake of it. They're descriptive words aimed at enlivening concepts.

Last thing on this audience. Publishers assume attention spans are at deficit levels, which they indulge through boxed elements scattered around the page in ever crazier configurations. Eventually, the page resembles more a post-festival campsite than anything likely to induce concentration in a student. Far better to use boxed content for something exceptional — such as an illustrative case study or a biography of a key protagonist — and to retain the centrality of the text. Narrative matters to this audience, so tell the story rather scatter it around the page.

(more on boxed content in Chapter Six).

f.   Potential customers

Another group requiring persuasion. In post-university sales training I was taught the mnemonic AIDA to recall the steps required to make a sale. Short for *Attention, Interest, Desire, Action*, they remain relevant for marketing and sales literature, whether for websites, brochures, written pitches or other forms of "collateral" (as it's known in the industry).

Design is important for *Attention*, which can leave the copywriter (the agency person that writes advertising content) competing with images and 80pt headlines at eccentric angles. The imagery usually takes precedence: most marketers believing passages of text incapable of winning the battle for consumers' attention. I've been presented with near-complete adverts on many occasions, with all the imagery decided by "creatives" and with the copywriter employed simply to fill in the (usually very small) textboxes — at this stage full of non-sensical Latin text (called *Lorem Ipsum* text in the industry).

I was once handed an advert for our PR firm with a food-processor chosen as the only vaguely relevant image of those available. Told to add the content, the best I could come up with was *The Right Blend for Your Company*, which was fine for new audiences but diluted our message to existing clients (of being their long-term specialist partner).

Yet the food-blender advert broke another cardinal rule: it was about us, not the target audience. Unless it's a car, a wristwatch or some gizmo, any sales copy should be about the reader rather than the product (in fact, it's mostly still true for cars and wristwatches). And this is especially the case when selling professional services.

This is the *Interest* element of the mnemonic. What dilemma currently obsesses the reader, or should do? What problems require an urgent solution, perhaps issues they didn't realise were about to disturb them? Pointing out dangers on the horizon is an important element of business writing no matter what the format, although it's especially pertinent when attracting potential customers.

As for *Desire* and *Action*: most copywriting guides will talk about keeping sentences short and using a variety of sentence structures (starting many with the object) — all of which is covered below. They will also talk about formulas such as "benefit, benefit, benefit" or "benefit/outcome", which is not covered below. And they will implore you to end on an action point, which is usually more than simply screaming "ACT NOW!" — and often involves something practical such as calling a freephone number or clicking a link.

But this isn't our world, except in one respect — perfectly captured by my favourite book on marketing. In *Marketers are From Mars, Consumers are from New Jersey*, "mad man" Bob Hoffman sets out his thesis that the advertising industry has lost touch with consumers: something it did around the same time it lost touch with reality, he claims. Worse, the industry doesn't seem to have noticed and, if it has, it doesn't care.

He attacks the industry from many angles, including its new-found addiction to "content" — a word he hates for describing both a "Shakespeare sonnet and a picture of my cat's ass". The word has become debased, he claims, suggesting a better description would be "web litter".

In part, this is due to the direction such content has taken in recent years. Advertisers no longer sell products, says Hoffman (pursuing his theme further in his *Ad Contrarian* blog), but "engage in the community" via blogs and social media channels that allow brands to "co-create with people". One result has been what's known as "shared purpose" marketing in which consumers are supposed to become fans of a brand or product, not because of its relevance or quality but due to a "like-mindedness with the customer".

Of course, this sounds like the audience-centric approach we'd want for our content. Only it isn't. The combination of short-attention delivery-channels such as *Twitter*, and a near-desperate need for advertisers to find something worth engaging with while avoiding the hard sell, results in messaging that ends up alienating as many people as it engages. Some "engagements" even end with companies screaming "and if you don't like what we have to say, you're welcome to shop elsewhere".

To be clear, the problem is rarely the underlying causes — many of which are laudable. It's the delivery via nuance-destroying quick-fire media channels, the hectoring tone of the "engagement" and, frankly, the hypocrisy of brands claiming the moral high-ground while avoiding taxes and pursuing profits in some of the least "shared purpose" countries globally.

Complex content, where the message matters, needs space. And if the "action point" of any advertising campaign is "please shop elsewhere," don't be surprised if that's exactly what your customers decide to do.

g.   The media

When starting out as a writer I thought editors the immovable gate-keepers to my ambitions. They were scary characters that could condemn my work at a glance and just as quickly dismiss me as a lost cause, barring me from ever crossing their threshold again.

Later on, I became an editor and saw the role differently. Now I thought it a stressful, under-appreciated, multi-tasking assignment in which the buck stopped with me no matter what the concern: all while trying to meet hard deadlines on a limited budget, and while juggling a range of intangibles involving less-than-reliable individuals.

As a frazzled editor the writers I appreciated were those that understood my needs and offered a solution. Those that submitted copy tailored to my readership; that was interesting, novel, well-written and formatted correctly (following our style guides regarding headlines, standfirst, bylines and spellings etc.). Especially welcome were writers offering to fill gaps in our coverage (maybe from specific regions), as were offers to help fill regular needs (regarding news or data, for instance).

Of course, the editor's power is much reduced, both by the advent of the internet — squeezing revenues for traditional media — and by the growth of social media, which created new (more immediate) forms of content distribution. Yet this is absolutely to the detriment of quality, in my view, meaning that — while writers should celebrate the expanded opportunities for being published, even if the chances of being remunerated well (or at all) have decreased — they should mourn that lost fear of the editor's red pen or spike. It made us all better writers.

Certainly, writing for the media should be the ambition for anyone reading this book. Books and white papers need promoting. And that's best done through "slicing and dicing" your content for different audiences via different (often specialist) publications. Generating 800- to 1200-word articles on particular themes — that help sell your greater wares — is also excellent practice, good fun and thoroughly rewarding.

It's always a thrill to see your byline and maybe a photo on a double-page spread showcasing your expertise. If no one else, your mum will love it. But it's important to get the approach right. Focus on that publication's intended audience and make sure that's how you pitch your article: as the very concern plumbers in the UK must know about, now! And they need to hear about it, not because you're brilliant or your company has got the answer (that's implicit), but because the changes to environmental regulations you're warning them about are going to hit those plumbers hard.

But do your research. If the publication you're pitching has just released *The Plumbers' Guide to the New Green Regulations*, you'll have to offer an angle that moves the debate forward.

4.   Who am I?

Now seems like a good moment for some background above and beyond that offered in the Preface. As the deputy editor and chief sub-editor of a magazine I acquired the moniker Bob the Butcher when dealing with copy, which I was secretly proud of though can see now how others may have perceived it negatively. The problem was that tens of thousands of words flowed across my desk every week — most of which failed to meet the magazine's most basic needs.

It wasn't rocket science. We were a specialist monthly magazine writing technical content for a discerning audience. Our readership was well-educated, engaged and global, with a high percentage using English as their second language. As well as the core news content, they also needed to learn about complex concepts that were mostly central to their immediate concern, though also sometimes tangential. We therefore had a wide brief but one requiring a narrow (or narrowing) interpretation. A particular lens, in other words, like most specialist titles.

Articles needed an obvious angle that was clearly stated, preferably at the top. They needed a well-ordered and logical structure. And they needed to stay on-topic. Given that we were a specialist title, they didn't even need to be that interesting, though they needed a compelling (non-hyperbolic) style that — supported by the structure — complemented the angle.

These are forgiving rules, capable of making pretty-average writing passable. Yet, week after week, month after month, I found myself printing out the verbiage on my scene, extracting the required facts, working out the angle, and rebuilding the entire article from scratch. On many occasions the only element the writers could instantly recognise was their byline — hence the nickname.

That was in the early 1990s. One would think I might have mellowed since, but I haven't — to the point that some assume I derive sadistic pleasure from destroying others' copy. Actually, I don't, though I do get a fantastic lift when young trainees graduate from what we call Writer's Boot Camp to start banging out articles that are clear, accurate, well-structured and written in a style that draws you in and keeps you reading, no matter how dry the subject.

And that's my justification for this book. I cannot regale readers with anecdotes about famous literary names or tales from the legendary titles of Fleet Street. My time as a wordsmith has been spent toiling in the unfashionable back alleys of professional content: crafting copy for the stiff world of business and finance, often to support practitioners with a need to communicate highly-esoteric complexities to an audience of peers.

Yet in every case the need for strong writing was made greater, not weaker, by the subjects being tackled. It was never florid prose that made the difference. It was an understanding of what was required of the content — most essentially for the audience we write for and why — as well as what that meant for the angle, the content, the structure and the style.

Communicating expertise

And it was this focus on strong audience-facing content that took me — after a short stint in banking — into the world of public relations. I had no experience in PR when I started my small agency. Not a jot. But I could see how the existing PR offering was failing my branch of the finance industry.

It was too fluffy, too shallow and too obsessed with knowing the right people. And it had no idea how to communicate the extraordinary expertise within some of the world's largest and most complex organisations. That was in 2002. The world has somewhat caught up with us since, although — given the number of ex-journos in PR — it still amazes me how little emphasis there is on using strong content to highlight their clients' expertise.

We had to produce razor-sharp content for some of the world's largest and most demanding institutions. It had to be bang-on-the-money in terms of accuracy, of course. But it also had to be authentically the client's voice, as well as avoid being a promotional puff-piece. Finally, it had to be turned around quickly and without fuss.

And we found training keen-as-mustard graduates easier than converting dyed-in-the-wool hacks. Time and again, highly experienced writers would turn in deeply disappointing articles requiring a rewrite. Meanwhile, the junior writers would quickly pick up writing for our audiences via Writer's Boot Camp, as well as how to pitch their work to editors (something the old hacks often thought beneath them).

Yes, I got a buzz out of Boot Camp. I've trained somewhere in the region of 100 writers, some now highly respected authors and (nearly) all capable of turning in great content. It's my proudest achievement.

Yet books have always been my first love, going right back to a book on *The Lost Villages of Essex* I wrote on my mother's portable typewriter after various bike rides as an awkward and isolated 12-year-old stuck in a rough comprehensive school.

That won me a write-up in the local newspaper, though it was never published. Nor were some half-finished novels, with my first published book (by *Transworld*) a *roman a clef* about my time as a single man in New York. It was the end of the 1990s and, I thought, a typical "lad-lit" offering.

Others thought differently, resulting in me spending much of the past 20 years apologising for both my poor (though exaggerated) dating etiquette while living in New York and the far-worse crime of actually writing about it. Still, it's there as a writing achievement: a published author by one of the world's largest publishing houses in my early-30s.

This was followed, after a ten-year gap, by a series of bestselling self-help books, now translated into ten or so languages. These include *What's Stopping You?*, *Get Things Done* and *The Outside Edge* (about achieving things as an outsider in a world made by insiders). These books deal with the mental barriers preventing people from achieving their goals or even setting goals worthy of themselves. And that includes contemplating major writing projects, making what I learnt researching those books (particularly *Get Things Done*) highly useful for the endeavour ahead.

Yet there are no miracles to reveal. There's no alchemy. It's about preparing ourselves mentally for the task to come, developing a process, doing the research, getting going and keeping at it despite the inevitable setbacks. We could call it *What's Stopping You Writing That Book?* Or *Get That White Paper Done*.

But it's worth the effort. Completed and published long-form writing projects are the route to personal fulfilment for those with something to say. They're also one of the mainstays of our civilisation: the building blocks of progress. Just ask Charles Darwin.

Chapter Two

The process of writing

1. Angle, content, structure, style

Writing's tough. It's a lonely pursuit, really only suitable for misanthropists and hermits. It involves hours of sitting in the same position, locked away, banging a keyboard. And all the while you might be completely wasting your time. Humiliating yourself, even.

But we knew that. And we're still here. So we need to put aside our doubts and get going, which involves — in my view — three core elements. It involves developing a process for writing. It involves motivation. And it requires discipline. This chapter will deal with all three, as well as one of our greatest hurdles once underway — the "condition" known as writer's block.

Yet, at this stage, it's process that matters most because if we get that right it'll aid motivation and help retain discipline.

Any writing project — whether a book, white paper or an article — has an order of execution. And it's the deviation from that order that triggers many of the worst problems as well as a good number of the outright failures. I've mentioned the order before, but here it becomes official, it's: *Angle, Content, Structure, Style*.

a.   Angle

What's your point? Your take? What view or line is being put forward? If you don't have an angle, you don't have a book (and you certainly don't have a white paper or article). The angle must run through the content like the word Brighton through a stick of rock — preferably through every paragraph and absolutely through every chapter or section.

Of course, the odd interesting aside is fine for illustrating a point or adding colour. Too many, and readers' minds will start to wander. A whole chapter dedicated to something other than the core angle and they'll think they're reading the wrong book — and it may well indicate you're pursuing the wrong angle.

b.   Content

Having discerned our angle, we need to establish what's in and what's out. All subjects can grow exponentially when researched, making this a critical editing task. For what's in we need to understand the depth and detail required for our book. For instance, does our village history require a description of every tombstone in the graveyard or just the main monuments? Every house around the village green, or just those of interest?

Equally, we need a view on what's rejected. If it wasn't relevant to the project's angle — fine. But what if it challenges the angle? Rejecting it could undermine the entire premise of the project. And, yes, the content-gathering part of the process might well result in an altered angle: better that than a book or white paper that's easily refuted.

c.   Structure

Good writers are generating draft structures from the moment the project is conceived. This could start with, say, four elements (for this book it was: why and what to write; the process of writing; elements of content; and style) that are then built out, with elements moved and added (for this chapter — on process — I added motivation and discipline and soon realised that overcoming barriers such as writer's block should also be included).

A draft and detailed table of contents is always in development — constantly being shaped and adapted during the content-gathering process. And when the writing begins, that table of contents will start changing again. Far from being a pain, this shaping and reshaping is critical for the creation of coherent and readable work. It will highlight gaps as well as potentially superfluous content. And once set — finally, long into the drafting process and possibly only when editing — the satisfaction of knowing that this is our strongest possible structure should give us confidence in our work.

Two things to note:

- This works equally well for just an article, with the four parts simply four sections (of four-five paragraphs each). Indeed, as we write each chapter of our book, or section of our white paper, we should apply the same process,
- Again, the angle is all-important. When deciding the structure, the angle should help discern both what content we include and the order of its presentation. After all, we're presenting a thesis while citing supportive evidence, so its architecture will directly impact its persuasiveness.

d. Style

While often the first thing we notice when reading a book, it should be the last thing we worry about when writing one. I don't mean last in importance — get this wrong and our life as a writer will be short. I mean that it's the final element of the process.

Decide the angle, research the content and build the structure. And then write it, perhaps with one eye on the chapter lengths (to keep them broadly in line). And then — and only then — focus on style. I've heard of writers that have failed to make progress beyond the first chapter — first page, even — after becoming obsessed with style. Forget style. At least for now.

Notice that style comes a long way down the table of contents for this book. That's because parts one, two and three of the process are all that matter until the final stage, and that includes what Ann Handley, in her 2014 book *Everybody Writes* calls, "The Ugly First Draft" (TUFD).

Every book I've written (or written successfully) I've written twice. Once to finalise the angle, content and structure. And once again to develop and hone the style and to progress beyond the TUFD. First drafts can be awful. Who cares? It's only in the second and third (or even fourth) iteration that we need to pay any attention to the readability of the piece or the consistency of the style.

Chapter One, I've found, nearly always needs an entire rewrite by the time I attack the final chapters. This is partly because new material has changed my approach to the angle — sometimes even altering it altogether. But mainly it's due to my style settling only around Chapter Three. From there I'm more fluid. I've found my voice, making me hate the earlier chapters (until they're rewritten, of course).

So, there it is: *Angle, Content, Structure, Style*. Like Handley's TUFD, I've been tempted to invent a mnemonic to help memorise this order: ACoSS perhaps, or ACESS with the inserted E standing for Edit or Evaluate, meaning that — once we have collated the content — we work out what's in and what's out. But that's making the hand fit the glove in my view (as mnemonics often do), hence why I've always preferred our trainees to simply remember those four words.

They drive home the critical message regarding the order of events. And that it's the corruption of that sequence — most commonly focusing too much or too early on style — that causes too many writing projects to fall over.

2. Motivation (or getting started)

Here's a classic writer's dilemma: what should be my first sentence? In fact, that was it because it was the first thing that came to me after creating a draft structure. I jotted it down, by hand, and two others quickly followed. I then typed them up in *Word*, and that triggered the next sentence. Soon I had a paragraph: this one.

That's the joy of structuring (and of word processing, of course). Here we are, halfway down Chapter Two with the above paragraph the first one written. We can write what we like when we like and it's not wasted from being out of sequence. Incomplete or floating sentences can be jotted down under various headings as they come to us, not as the order of the book dictates. It's a lot easier and more fun than starting at Chapter One, line one, and ending at the final line of the final chapter.

It makes me admire the likes of George Orwell and Ernest Hemingway all the more. Typing on a *Remington* or something equally manual — with any corrections both interruptive and messy — they had to type in the right order, starting at page one and ending at *The End*. Of course, it wasn't quite like that. But life's a lot easier with word processing that's for sure.

What's this got to do with motivation? Everything. Just as the hardest part of going to the gym is walking through the front door, so the hardest part of writing is getting started. Though it's also repeating that start. Just as our triumph over the gym door lasts only for a single visit, so does starting that writing session last only that one session. These are single-use victories. Tomorrow, the battle begins again.

When reluctant to visit the gym, I'll convince myself with the thought I could simply lie in the *Jacuzzi* or do some gentle cycling. Just walk through the door, I'll say to myself. Just get changed. Just do a few minutes on the cross-trainer. All in an effort to cross the threshold — knowing that, once in, I'll want to first earn that soak.

Writing's no different. Just sit at your desk. Just switch on that laptop or PC. Just open the *Word* document. Whatever mental bargains it takes to make that first move, make them. Because that book (or white paper or article) won't write itself, which is a line I often use when chastising myself for procrastination.

The cockpit for our journey

Of course, starting is a lot easier when we've created the right environment for writing. And that involves our writing desk or workstation (to use the more functional modern descriptor). This is the cockpit for our writing journey. The place where we succeed or fail — making it critically important that it's set up for success. It doesn't have to be a wood-panelled writer's garret or a fashionable shed in the garden (though both would be nice). But it does have to be somewhere we want to spend time. Lots of time.

Some tips on creating that writer's lair we've always dreamt of:

- Make it as soundproof as possible — somewhere away from the children's playroom or noisy kitchen. The near-mythical kitchen table as a writer's desk is a recipe for disruption and is really only for those with no other choice. Dining rooms are better (and come with a big desk) but not if you have to clear the table for dinner every night. Spare bedrooms — especially a long way from others — are fantastic but will obviously need a desk. Sheds are also great, but not if there's a concern over weatherproofing or power or cold drafts or heating or the wifi,

- And yes, it should be a permanent space. Writing is a repeat exercise in which you must enter the same mental space every day. Starbucks with a laptop is a poor substitute, although some prefer it. For some writers, the café — particularly a favourite spot within it — helps with inspiration. Fine, for when inspiration is required (maybe to overcome writer's block). When it comes to the hard yards of drafting, however, constant distractions are likely to kill concentration,

- And Starbucks is never going to afford you the expanse of silence required. That said, even that posh writing shed will have trouble blocking out the three O'clock flight from Chicago, making access to background-blocking music a necessity. The music should be familiar (this is no time to explore new genres) and repetitive (instrumentals are best). It should also avoid the highs and lows that can become disturbing. For instance, I'm writing this listening to Verdi's *La traviata*. It's music I love and know, so it doesn't disturb my thought patterns and helps block-out my children shouting at screens while playing *Minecraft* or the dog barking at yet another delivery. Yet classical music, including opera — while inspirational — can rise and fall, especially as the inevitable Act III denouement approaches. These can crash into your consciousness, even if familiar. So I regularly fall back on the "concentration music" compilations found on *YouTube* and *Spotify*,

- Headphones might be required for very noisy environments, though I find any headphones uncomfortable if worn for too long. Some decent speakers could also be a good investment and are certainly better than relying on your PC or laptop speaker — not least because you can place them as a sound barrier between you and the source of noise (usually a door or window),

- Invest in the right equipment. Laptops are the norm these days, although I'm writing this on an old PC because I prefer the bigger screen and the chunkier keyboard (both of which can be attached to a laptop). It doesn't have to be the most expensive designer Mac. It just needs *Word* (though fancier writing software exists). And an *Inkjet* printer will do. But there are those that like buying "the gear" because it encourages them to use it. Fine: all encouragements welcome,

- You also need: a desk large enough for your laptop/PC as well as your notes; reference books and dictionaries; an ergonomically efficient chair — office chairs can be as cheap as £50 and are better for your back than a borrowed kitchen chair; somewhere to stash the books and files that make up your content (assuming they're not all electronic); and a stand for the printer,

- Buy lots of stationery. Tech-heads will tell you this is unnecessary but, in my view, the right stationery is essential for all sorts of reasons, including getting going, overcoming procrastination, jotting down thoughts and beating writer's block. Stationery preferences are personal, though mine include an A4 ruled hardcover notebook (something that will survive train journeys and coffee spills), though a classic Moleskine will most certainly do; a pocket-sized (A6 or A7) notebook to have with you always; loose 6x4 inch indexing cards; A4 paper for the printer; and some decent biros and ballpoints. These are the essentials in my view (serious writers do not take notes on their iPhone). Whatever your preference, notebooks should always be nearby, even next to the bed for those half-awake moments when the best lines surface.

Stationery matters most when starting. This section began with me jotting down a potential opening sentence — by hand, in a notebook. And that's how we should start now. While writing habits differ, I find an empty page of an A4 notebook far more enticing at the start of a writing project than a blank *Word* file on a screen.

Ruled or unruled — it doesn't matter. The point is to not feel restricted by an electronic page that will record words, one-after-the-other, in a straight line. That's where the blockages can start. So just jot down words — anywhere on the page, and in any order — that start the thinking process for your project.

As stated, the genesis of this book was a *PowerPoint* presentation for new employees, which — as well as offering a ready-made structure (since modified) — provides another potential starting point if pens and notebooks grate. Without the necessities of correct grammar and pleasing syntax, the words come more easily. So open *PowerPoint* and write some bullets.

For instance. My random bullets could run as follows:

- How to write non-fiction,
- Non-fiction = books, white papers, articles, blogs,
- For professionals and would-be writers,
- Not just style — process,
- Other elements: openings, endings, formatting, graphs,
- Overcoming barriers.

With the audience and a provisional angle decided, the core elements of the content are starting to fall into place. And there's even a nascent structure. Importantly, style is being completely ignored — banished as a concern until much later on.

It's all about *flow*

I've written whole chapters by hand before typing them up — editing as I go. It's that all-important *flow* that matters, allowing me to get into my stride and stay there as long as possible.

Flow? Writers such as Daniel Goleman, Daniel H. Pink and Charles Duhigg have all written about *flow*, though the concept is at-tributed to psychologist Mihály Csíkszentmihályi. *Flow* is the optimal psychological state for learning. It's where both the challenge and your response are stretched but aligned: in balance and highly productive. It's an intense and immersive focus where time disappears. First noticed in athletes, the concept is also highly relevant to creativity — in fact anything requiring concentration, endeavour and craft (Goleman uses the example of Joe Kramer, a railroad repair-yard welder).

Csíkszentmihályi contrasts it to the state of *anxiety*, which is usually a result of low skill levels being tasked with a challenge perceived as too great; and the state of *relaxation*, in which the skill level is way higher than the challenge. Both *anxiety* and *relaxation* are recipes for procrastination and distraction, and ultimately failure. For success, *flow's* the required state.

Tackling procrastination

Thanks to procrastination, an idea can swirl around in our head or remain stuck in a notebook for years before we actually write it down. This is the habit of deferring or delaying action: the "maybe tomorrow" thought that nags away though is never quite urgent enough to be tackled.

Experts such as Jane B. Burka and Lonara M. Yuen, in their seminal book called *Procrastination* (1983), are at pains to point out that this isn't laziness or even lack of discipline. Its roots "involve inner feelings, fears, hopes, memories, dreams, doubts and pressures". It might be a sign of low self-esteem — that we feel unworthy of the project before us and therefore find excuses for delaying its execution.

Burka and Yuen call this the Procrastinator's Code — fear-generated thinking that produces a desire to consciously or unconsciously delay taking action.

"Many people who procrastinate are apprehensive about being judged by others or by the critic who dwells within," they write. Regret, irritation, self-condemnation and despair can all follow: all unhelpful states for approaching a writing project.

A related aspect is perfectionism, with the procrastinator convinced that what they produce must be perfect or it isn't worth starting. Perfectionists assume their skills must be applied easily — be an innate talent — so that any effort, even something requiring editing, condemns them to the mediocrity that their inner self is convinced is their fate.

Of course, Burka and Yuen are professionals (from the University of California) so their cure for procrastination involves reconditioning the mind — including reconciling childhood experiences to encourage new neural conditioning. We don't have that much time and we're simply trying to execute a writing project. We must therefore steel ourselves for the task ahead, although also remember the order of events and that style — the main source of procrastinator angst — comes last, meaning we can comfort ourselves by making progress on the other elements.

3. Discipline (or keeping going)

Yet starting a writing project is a walk in the park compared to finding the discipline to keep going. The road ahead is daunting. It's also full of potholes, steep inclines and confusing junctions. No wonder so many half-finished books languish in forgotten folders within junked PCs and laptops.

Whenever I start a new writing project I'm haunted by the Pink Floyd song *Time*, from *Dark Side of the Moon*, and particularly the line "plans that either come to naught or half a page of scribbled lines". Like most writers, I've dozens of them. So how do we prevent this project from becoming yet another casualty? This is perhaps the toughest assignment in this book: instilling within the writer the discipline to keep going despite the doubts, the setbacks, the mental blocks and the distractions.

And then there's the fact we're all different. What works for some won't work for others. But there are nonetheless habits that are effective when it comes to the discipline required to complete a major writing project (or even a minor one). I think there are seven: *7 Habits for Highly Disciplined Writers*. And, yes, they do take inspiration from Stephen Covey's *The 7 Habits of Highly Effective People*, among others.

1. **KBO.** This was Winston Churchill's mantra to himself, especially in his "wilderness years" before 1940. It stands for "keep buggering on" — a profane expression and a little dated but one that means a lot more than simply "keep going". It's acknowledging the mundanity, the boredom, the frustrations, the barriers and even the pain. Writing is all that. But we just need to keep moving forward, putting one word in front of another. Again and again. Until it's done. This makes KBO a reasonable mantra, perhaps when reluctant to start a session.

   Yet KBO can seem inappropriate to modern sensitivities, so why not adopt my writing mantra of "it won't write itself"? Or how about the word "onward" for those seeking something more inspiring? Whatever it is, find a mantra — a phrase or word that tells you to "get on it" and "stay on it".

2. **Plan.** This is a straight lift from Covey, whose second habit is "begin with the end in mind". Too many book failures are caused by the writer having a strong idea how to start a writing project but little idea how to continue. The reason is simple — the overall shape of the book is not apparent to them from the outset. So, while a somewhat repeated point (and there are repetitions ahead because repetition helps), the importance of developing a cogent structure cannot be overstated.

Of course, there are those with the opposite problem. They cannot start, which we've dealt with above and will deal with below. Yet this is about keeping going, which — with good structuring and planning — is simply a case of filling in the blanks under our headings or continuing a journey towards an agreed destination. Think of your project as a train heading for Edinburgh. We've a firm idea of the end — the Scottish capital — but equal clarity regarding the stops along the way: Peterborough, Doncaster, York and Newcastle. Each stop has its own character while being part of the whole. And, importantly, we're thinking about the entire journey from the start while focusing on the next station.

This section's easy — I've seven habits that need writing (a ready-made plan). But any section should follow a similar pattern. For instance, my "why write" opening began with a list:

- Something to say,
- Expertise to communicate,
- A gap that needs filling,
- Shaping ideas,
- A craft not a talent.

Sure, it became corrupted in the writing but that was all I needed to give me the framework to start, to keep going, and to finish.

3. **Number.** Another Covey lift. His third habit is "first things first", meaning generate an order. My version is to number sections, not just chapters but also within each chapter. Those numbers you see are for me — the writer — not you, the reader (and can be removed in the final edit). They denote headings that start as no more than a list of words. They order my thoughts while also telling me where to file tangential thoughts before I can get to them.

Numbering also allows my notes from researching the content to be transferred to the *Word* file under various headings, perhaps just as jotted notes ("element on [XXX] here") before any attempt at turning them into cogent passages. The point is they're no longer random or just in my head. They have a home, on a page, under a number — and we'll get to them when we're ready.

4. **Focus.** By this I mean focus on one chapter at a time. Let it obsess you. It should be in your head for the entire period it's being drafted. As it expands — from jotted words to numbered headings and from bullets to sentences and paragraphs — you should be thinking constantly about what to include and how to improve it. When showering, when walking the dog, when doing your day job: think about *this* chapter. That way, your reticular activating system (RAS) kicks in and offers thoughts and ideas that you'd never expected to conjure. Your RAS? It's the function within your brain alerting you to what's important while filtering out what isn't. Ever noticed that, when thinking about buying a new car (as one example), there are suddenly more models of that car around than you'd previously realised? That's your RAS. Of course, other thoughts will crash the party: about different sections or maybe ideas for a whole new section. Fine, but they belong in the notebook or under a numbered heading. What matters now is *this* chapter. And this one alone.

5. **Schedule.** It makes sense to follow your natural rhythm of alertness and creativity and to schedule your writing time accordingly. I'm an early writer, sharpest in the morning. So I try and push back calls and meetings until at least mid-morn-

ing. Yet it's not when I'm at my most creative, which is usually in the evening when more relaxed. If possible, I schedule two one-hour sessions a day: the first to write furiously to cover the ground; the second to revisit the same ground more creatively, including the first take on sense, style and accuracy.

Those sessions are in the diary. They mean a lot to me. I'd even say I'm addicted: needing to write from 7.30-8.30, both am and pm. Certainly, I can act like an addict when I'm denied my fix because there's a meeting or a dinner, or a household chore that needs doing.

Nothing instils discipline like allocated time for the task. Scheduled time that's ignored nags at the conscience and harms our self-esteem. Meanwhile, a completed and productive session releases feel-good hormones and boosts our sense of well-being. It also helps us focus on the day job.

Since 2002, I've also kept a diary and so should you. Mine's an A5 hardback diary, though I realise they're increasingly dated. What's important is the idea of keeping a daily journal: one that records what you're going to write, and when, and also how you found writing it. It's amazing how many further thoughts appear as you do.

6. **Overlap.** Never end one session without knowing where the next one starts. The aim is to overcome the most common cause of an abandoned book: not knowing how Chapter Two (or Part Two), or Three or Four, begins. Because they're far easier to pick up again after a rest, sessions are therefore best left halfway through one element. Your mind will be full of the need to complete it — buzzing with ideas. Meanwhile, a closed chapter can feel like a finished book. As a

writer, you can feel lost. Unsure what's next. Far better to start afresh mid-session, allowing you to break while firmly ensconced within.

Yet there's an obvious flaw in this method: that sessions ending halfway through a chapter/section can feel like an abrupt halt to your thinking — a *coitus interruptus* for your creativity. This can be soothed by the differing needs required for different stages of production. The famous *flow* required when writing — with the juices flowing and the words pouring forth onto the page — should not be interrupted, of course. But that's not the point being made. As discussed, each chapter also needs planning and structuring, which could be the final job before breaking — making a strong session one that's divided into two parts: starting with writing (the chapter/section requiring your focus) and ending with planning/ structuring (the next chapter or section requiring your focus).

That way, you're tripping over each chapter's threshold and avoiding the mental hill-climbs required when staring at the heading Chapter [X].

A last point on this: I always note my stop by typing HERE in capitals. It tells me that a chain-link has been opened that needs to be closed. And on those occasions where I'm keen to jump ahead it acts as a marker for my return so that each chapter — while under construction — can contain several HERE points awaiting completion.

7. **100-MORE**. I've targeted 7000 words per chapter and I'm now on 6700 (yes, part four below was written earlier). There's 300 to go, which is doable in this session. I've just ignored an incoming phone call and turned on some concentration music to avoid any distrac-

tions. Around 250 to go now. Yes, I agree, this is a daft way to write a book — it's more like a reluctant adolescent completing a homework assignment. But it's not a bad way to instil some discipline. Personal trainers know that the "come on, ten more" cry — with 100 push-ups already complete — is a great way of adding incremental capacity to their client's exercise regime. So the "come on, 100 more words" can do the same for a writer (fewer than 200 now).

As stated, writing is an exercise in putting one word in front of another. But that's hard work. The more we can stretch our word output per session, when already at our desks and with the thoughts flowing — and with 1000 words or so already under our belts — then the farther along the 50,000 word-path we can progress.

And we can even do this against the clock. For instance, it's now 8.25, so this session needs to close. But I think, with the right focus, I can reach that wordcount by 8.30. Of course, we have the "overlap" element to come — the planning and sketching for the next session. But that's just the classic "warm-down" (to maintain the personal-trainer analogy). There's not the same need to stretch sinews and concentrate hard to complete the last few yards of sentence construction. And, no, I'm not concerned by style. Nor grammar. That comes later. It's just those last 10-or-so words until the finish line. Done.

4. Overcoming writer's block

It's not easy. We've established that. Starting is hard. Staying disciplined even harder. And then there's writer's block, which can disable us even when motivated and disciplined. Sometimes, the words simply won't come. What then?

Few writers possess the stamina to pitch-up in front of a screen and continuously type away until their book or white paper is finished, although there are some famous exceptions — of books written in an almost single continuous *flow*. These include Robert Louis Stephenson's *The Strange Case of Dr Jekyll and Mr Hyde* (three days) and *The Boy in the Striped Pyjamas*, John Boyne (2.5 days).

Yet note that both are fiction, meaning the writer could load up on caffeine (or stronger substances) and let rip. It was all in their heads — just needing a creativity-riot and brain dump onto the page. The nature of non-fiction makes this impossible. We're communicating our research or expertise and constructing an argument, so a brain dump won't cut it, at least not without some serious editing to ensure the relevance, veracity and logical coherence of our output. Breaks are inevitable, which means episodes of writer's block are also likely because they generally occur at the start of a new session.

This is less a moment when a writer simply stares at a blank screen and is unable to start, perhaps akin to *dartitis* (a condition experienced by darts players, resulting in them being unable to let go of the dart — a similar condition in golf being the yips). It's more akin to a car that won't start. Despite the motor turning over and there being plenty of fuel, something isn't firing up.

Yes, there are some *dartitis*-type moments when not a single word will come out, though — more commonly — it's that every start seems false: wooden, insincere, stupid. In previous eras the result would have been scrunched papers littering the floor. These days, sentences on a screen are written and written-over again and again. Nothing works. *Word* remains open. And blank.

The most likely result is an abandoned session. Today's not the day, you reason — so let's go for a bike ride or bake a cake. Fine, but this is probably the most dangerous moment in any writer's life. Abandon the task once and it's a lost session. Twice, and it's starting to look like a habit. Three times, and perhaps the entire project has lost its allure.

It can even lead to a harsh retrospective. Your view of previously written chapters can change until you're soon staring at a body of work that, for the first time, feels truly and utterly shit. Baking cakes now seems far more enjoyable or cycling just what's needed to lose some of the weight gained from all those wasted sedentary hours writing.

At this point you're no longer a writer, which is quite a price to pay for a momentary false start at the beginning of a writing session. And it's a price worth avoiding.

Some tips:

- Never abandon the session. Instead, abandon the word processor. Eye strain could be doing as much harm to you mentally as it is to your eyesight. Take out that A4 lined and bound notepad, a nice ballpoint pen, and write by hand. And if the sentences won't come just scribble some notes,

- And if reverting to a pen and notebook doesn't work try writing a list of "elements to include" on a 6x4 indexing card (or similar) — or even on screen if you're up to it. Perhaps today is a day for structuring new chapters or maybe checking the content rather than writing,

- Or think about an entirely different section. This is helped by our building-block approach to structuring and drafting. With four to five discrete elements to consider, it might just be that your attention is already wandering on. So, this once, indulge it by starting part two or three. Notes or bullets are all that's needed at this stage, though you may manage a few sentences on a fresh topic,

- If not wanting to abandon the word processer, write a letter (or these days an email) to someone about your writer's block. Explain the problem to them. It could be a friend or even your mum. But it shouldn't be someone you see as a potential reader. It might just be that the change of audience is enough to start the right words rolling. Also, you're writing to them personally. Syntax, style, grammar etc. are not important. Nor are the facts: it's the telling of the dilemma that matters. Probably, you should not send the letter (though your mum might appreciate it, nonetheless),

- Think that's silly? Then write to a colleague, perhaps asking for advice about how to explain a particular element. Again, asking the question changes the perspective: it's now you seeking rather than offering advice, which might unlock the words required to start,

- Change room or, better still, change the environment altogether. J.K. Rowling wrote the early Harry Potter books in a café (The Elephant House in Edinburgh). The London Library in St. James's Square was the preferred writing location for many famous writers (Joseph Conrad, Rudyard Kipling, Agatha Christie, Edith Sitwell, Virginia Woolf, E.M. Forster, John Betjeman, Siegfried Sassoon, to name just a few). Perhaps a session in a café or library will, again just this once, give you the change of scene required,

- Finally, if none of that works, go for a walk or a bike ride, but stay local in case the inspiration returns. And take a pocket notebook and pen.

The two final options open up an important need for avoiding writer's block, which is the mental warm-up. Just as the journey to the library or café can help stimulate your thoughts for the session ahead (so much so that you should be bursting with thoughts by the time you arrive), so we can replicate that feeling when working in the back bedroom or shed.

Professional sportspeople warm up and so should you. Don't sit at your desk first thing — walk the dog or do some sit-ups. Anything that gets the blood flowing and allows you to clear a mental space for thinking about what to write.

And you don't need to think linearly. For instance, what's the key thing that needs communicating in this section of the draft? Perhaps that's where to start — building the paragraphs before and after around it. Or maybe it's the ending, or the trickiest concept to explain (or the easiest). Anything but line one, because that's where the blockage seems to be.

Ultimately, of course, the only known cure for writer's block is to start writing. So perhaps — when all's said and done — we just need to remember that our book (or white paper or article) won't write itself.

KBO!

Chapter Three

The elements of non-fiction

Quick question: did the order of Chapter One strike you as strange or unnatural in any way — perhaps a little forced? I hope not too forced but, if it did, the likelihood is that you detected it being written piece-meal and then stitched together in the editing process.

Apologies for my poor stitching, in that case. Yet the piecemeal or building-blocks approach is perfectly normal. In fact, it's to be encouraged because it allows us to write what we like when we like — not just to suit our moods or rhythms (though that too) but to deal with the fact that our thoughts are not linear.

Ideas can appear from different directions at random times and we should write them down and include them as and when they arrive. Of course, notebooks help. But there are times we'll want to attack a key element there and then and the building-blocks approach allows us to do that, aided by the early development of a numbered table of contents.

The next two chapters focus on this approach.

What do we mean by a building block? That depends. The chapters in this book average 7000 words — too large to be considered one block. Chapters of 1500 words or less could be treated as such, though even here breaking it down to 500-word sections will make it more digestible, especially for white papers totalling 3000 words or more.

What's important is that each block covers a discrete topic, perhaps divided by a "crosshead" sub-heading (see below). And that we consider these subjects to the exclusion of every other thought. We obsess about them, with any diverted thoughts towards other topics banished to notebooks or noted under the numbered headings in the *Word* document.

And when we can't ignore them? Well, that's just our brain telling us we're focusing on the wrong thing, which the building-blocks approach can accommodate.

In the next chapter we'll develop the blocks. Here, our goal is to focus on the elements that make up that block or can be added to any chapter or section. Each is important in its own way. And together they make up the whole.

1.　Body copy

Flour in a cake. Brick courses in a wall. Perhaps even the tarmac on the road or the water in a river? Whatever the analogy: the body copy or body text is the central element of our writing, making everything else decoration or furniture. It's there to convey our thoughts, ideas and opinions, as well as to narrate the journey between them.

It therefore needs to be simple. We're not writing prose or poetry. Sure, it needs rhythm and cadence, which we'll get to. But the objective is to relay information using the written word, which means it must be easily and immediately understood by the reader. Their eye must cruise smoothly along the lines of text uninterrupted by reader snags.

Readers dislike becoming entangled in mangled phraseology or overblown hyperbole or words chosen for effect rather than clarity, all forcing them to reread a passage or continue reading despite becoming mystified. Meanwhile, readers like words they don't have to look up and concepts that make immediate sense no matter how complex.

All of which is your challenge as a writer: to develop body copy that simplifies and educates. That wins people over not turns people off. And that does so immediately — not after repeated re-readings.

Narrative is the answer. The telling of a story. This doesn't mean inventing characters and dialogue. But it does mean using the body copy to develop a plot. No matter what the information being conveyed it will have a story — context — that forms the journey to this point in time.

Even new regulations or scientific experiments are moments that have not occurred in isolation. So bring your reader to the threshold of this discovery and then take them across it before telling them what this could mean for the future. Don't start at the front door — or, at least, only start at the front door as a dramatic opening before adding context.

The body copy is made up of paragraphs, sentences and words, which we'll deal with below. But it also has to be seen as part of a whole. The body copy's style is therefore critical. We must develop a style and make that style consistent throughout. Successful writers encourage readers to fall in with their style: its pace and intonation and in some cases even its accent. It's sharp changes in style, perhaps from humorous to deadly serious or from breezy to densely technical — or even from wordy to taut — that will confuse and annoy readers.

(Chapter Five is dedicated to developing your voice as a writer).

2. Paragraphs

As a nightshift sub-editor on a weekly newspaper I worked alongside a page-editor who instructed me to use paragraph breaks to make the text fit the page. Some paragraphs (known as "paras" in the trade or even "pars") would become great blocks of text six inches tall while others were reduced to a single sentence. It didn't matter, he said. What mattered was getting through the nightshift in good time.

As his junior, and new, I followed his rule. But I immediately hated it. We were abusing the writer while taking the reader for granted — not caring about how we served up passages they'd taken time to write or paid good money to read. It felt like offering a restaurant meal — cooked by a qualified chef — with the food thrown randomly on the plate. Sure, the food's the same but the enjoyment's hugely diminished.

I soon ignored him. His concern was making the text fit the allocated space as well as eliminating widows and orphans (one-line paragraph endings at the top of a page, or one-line paragraph openings at the bottom). But I'd rather edit them out through tighter writing (rarely looser) than by messing with the integrity of the paragraph.

But it does point to a problem. Should paragraphs be discrete passages concerned with a single element? Or should they be breaks in the text — there to give the reader a breather and to inject "white space" onto the page (white space often being compared to oxygen by editors — allowing the page "to breathe").

To me, they're absolutely the former with the latter a happy accident aided by the fact paragraphs should be short. For most writing formats the perfect paragraph is somewhere between 70 and 110 words and/or four to five sentences. For books, this can be a little longer, for newspaper articles a little shorter (the difference being the expected attention-span of the reader). And, yes, this is a change from the days when book paragraphs, in particular, could run on over several pages.

But each should deal with a different topic. Here, para one is an anecdote about sub-editing copy, para two disagreed with the page editor's methods, and three the fact I ignored him in favour of editing content to fit the page design. Para four highlights the conflicting needs of a para, with para five offering a resolution. Para six (this one) demonstrates the differences — and on we go …

Just as readers expect the current sentence to follow on logically from the previous one, they're entitled to expect the same from each paragraph. Otherwise, you're asking your reader to unravel enigmas within your work, which (James Joyce wannabes please note) will tire and even bore them.

"Every paragraph should amplify the one that preceded it," says William Zinsser in his landmark work *On Writing Well*. Zinsser (whose thoughts infuse the pages ahead) also implores us to take special care with the last sentence of each paragraph because "it's the crucial springboard to the next paragraph".

This is part of the stitching that we shall come to in Chapter Four although here we need to address its potential contradiction with another requirement of the paragraph: that it should be a moveable block of text. Paragraphs should be capable of being reordered without rendering the text unreadable. If para three reads better under para five it should go there, with paras two and four still making sense when run in sequence. All of which underlines the need for paras to be discrete passages although the stitching or segues between them may change. That said, this is just as apt for blocks of paras, perhaps divided by a crosshead (see below).

A last point on paras. Search-engine optimisation specialists insist that online text carries paras often no longer than a single sentence (which explains the style of online newspapers such as *Buzzfeed* or *MailOnline*). Fine, if writing for online click-bait "news" outlets. For anything else it's the writing that matters and repeated single-sentence paras will disorientate the reader.

3.   Sentences

Short ones are best. Hemingway was famous for them. "Courage is grace under pressure," is probably his most famous (written in a letter to

F. Scott Fitzgerald). It's packed with meaning, contains no punctuation or sub-clausing — unlike this one — and is entirely self-standing in that it requires no further context to be understood.

Such powerful sentences are rare. But they're always worth seeking out. And, yes, they can become one-sentence paragraphs if they merit the space around them and stack-up as a standalone statement.

The point is simplicity: using plain English to draft understandable sentences. We should be addicted to them. Instead, we seem addicted to the clutter and pomposity of commercial or technocratic jargon. We think it makes us sound important. Learned. Perhaps worthy of a higher hourly rate.

Yet it alienates readers in droves and is a sure sign of our insecurity as a writer (and maybe as a professional). Those that rise above their professions and appeal to a wider audience rise above its jargon. They're the explainers: a strong underlying motive for writing non-fiction for many and one that makes them the leaders in their field.

Zinsser compares a pilot telling his passengers that he's "presently anticipating experiencing considerable precipitation" with the term "it may rain". The second sounds too simple but it's superior to the first in every other way. It's memorable, meaningful, precise, and just three words: allowing useful information to be communicated as efficiently as possible.

With strong structuring and accurate signposting (see headlines and crossheads below), our final edits should come down to rewriting our sentences to make them more concise. They should also be styled for consistency (see Chapter Five) and checked for accuracy. And where possible turned into something as compelling as Hemingway's opener above.

One trick: play around with sentence structure. Try starting with the object or the subject or the verb — and read them aloud to sound out the most compelling order.

Inverting sentences can make them more compelling.

For more compelling sentences, invert them.

The second reads like someone grabbing you by the collar to make their point, though it's a trick that wears with repetition. That said, there's certainly room for one inversion per para. And, as long as it's an additional point being made, beginning the final sentence of alternate paras with the word "and" can also prevent the reader's attention from wandering (as can starting paras that way).

And finally, sentences do not have to be grammatical. Their role is to make a point. Clearly. To be understood. Sentence construction involving a subject, an object and a verb is therefore unnecessary. Rules regarding split infinitives — as well as other absurdities such as not ending with a preposition — can also be entirely dispensed with.

Writing isn't a straight-jacket. That said, like a jazz musician or an abstract painter, breaking the rules will be a more artful exercise when you understand the rules being broken.

And being ungrammatical is not the same as being careless. Each sentence should pass the Hemingway test (of being as short, concise and as meaningful as possible) and avoid obvious errors such as confused tenses or pronouns. Or being cluttered with sub-clausing or overly punctuated.

If sentences are the brick courses of our construction, they should be pleasing to the eye and admired for their symmetry.

4.   Words

What of the bricks themselves? They're important. So important that Sir Ernest Gowers, when president of the English Association, was invited by the UK's HM Treasury to write his landmark book *The Com-*

plete Plain Words (1954). The ministry commissioned Gowers after becoming concerned about the declining use of language by officials.

Civil servants had become too "wordy" (not their word) when writing official documents: more concerned by sounding authoritative (i.e. self-important) than being understood. Many were using words to hide or obscure meaning rather than to explain — to obfuscate rather than enlighten — which was having a debilitating impact on relationships across Whitehall (the street in London housing many government ministries).

They turned to Gowers, who'd published a book called *Plain Words* in 1948 and had first written complaining about overly complex bureaucratic language in 1929. And he turned to former *Observer* editor and legendary man of letters Ivor Brown to introduce the subject.

"The craftsman is proud and careful of his tools: the surgeon does not operate with an old razor blade: the sportsman fusses happily and long over the choice of rod, gun, club or racquet. But the man who is working in words, unless he is a professional writer (and not always then), is singularly neglectful of his instruments."

Brown's quote fails the test of time in many respects, and we'll talk further regarding the real tools of a writer's trade. But the point is made: the words we use matter.

For Sir Ernest (and the Treasury), the enemy was the tendency for civil servants to use the most complicated language possible rather than the simplest. Brown called it "jargantuan" language or the "barnacular" while Gowers pointed out that Americans called it "gobbledygook". Today, we call it corporate jargon or buzzwords and even play "bullshit bingo" for when people are asked to *synergise* or to *reach out* for *low-hanging fruit*.

Both Gowers (who died in 1966) and Brown (1974) would be horrified at how the disease they fought valiantly to eradicate has so taken over our lives. Yet, we must remember, this is the language of the little people. The box-tickers. Just as those Treasury officials were using complex language to shield themselves from scrutiny — as a means to guard their tiny intellectual empires — so we can use language to do the opposite. To expand understanding, not restrict it to the *cognoscenti*. And words are the weapons we use to do so.

Short words are not necessarily better than long ones, though they usually are. Yet readily understood words are far superior to any word requiring your target reader to reach for a dictionary — probably the most hard-stop reader-snag of all.

If not a bureaucrat actively trying to confuse (or stay compliant, if being generous), the propensity for using obscure words is often viewed as arrogance or boastfulness in the writer. Yet I see it as a sign of inse-curity. Of imposter syndrome. Overly complex words are for people trying to prove their standing rather than improve understanding.

(there's more on corporate language in Chapter Five)

Adjectives, pleonasms and tautologies

Adjectives (descriptive attributes to a noun) tend to fare badly in any writing-style guide. Unsurprisingly Gowers hated them. Zinss-er dealt with them under "clutter" and even Keith Waterhouse, who wrote *the* book for British tabloid journalists called *Waterhouse on Newspaper Style* (1989) was circumspect regarding their use: "smother-ing an intro in a ketchup of adjectives does little to improve its flavour" was his verdict while noting how many of them — in tabloid journalism at least — are both clichéd and redundant (deaths are always grim, clues vital and murders brutal so why add them, he asks).

Our addiction to adjectives comes from the apparent need to add "colour" — that elusive substance bad writers think involves breath-less hyperbole and exaggeration or even just unnecessary emphasis. Yet adding adjectives is like using too much icing on a cake: it either masks a poorly-made sponge or, more likely, ruins a well-made one.

When subbing, I kill every *very* or *extraordinary* or other unnecessary emphasiser that provides no further information. If emphasis is a must, I tell them to find a better descriptor.

For instance, if something is difficult the word *very* pulls us no further along the difficulty scale because the scale's attributes are unknown. Meanwhile, knowing why something is difficult — that it is *exhausting* or *complex* or *strenuous* or *irritating* or *expensive* — helps the reader both contextualise and visualise the content, which keeps them interested.

Pleonasms are a lesser crime. Words added to nouns and verbs that repeat what's already been described, they're both forgivable, given their commonality, while revealing as a sign of loose writing. *Weather conditions* (weather), *strike action* (strike), *track record* (record), *sales event* (sales) are examples listed in *The Economist Style Guide* (the bible of such things), though there are many more (many).

Less admissible are tautologies. Our modern addiction to acronyms provides scope for some howlers: ATM *machine*, PIN *number*, GPS *system*, 3pm *in the afternoon*. Although there are many ways to trip up on a tautology — from the *evening sunset* to the *hot water heater* to the *tall skyscraper* — they're everywhere we look.

And this can extend to entire phrases. Gowers' *bête noire* was "the reason for this is because", which should be "this is because". Another was "the subject of the talk will be about" rather than "the talk is about". In each case the rule is obvious: cut out superfluous words, whether adjectives, verbs, adverbs or any other clutter. All should go.

But how can we tell what's clutter? Zinsser passes on the device of adding brackets around the words within a sentence that are not doing "useful work". If the sentence still makes sense without that preposition or adjective, round the brackets go, which is the prelude to an extraction unless we feel it deeply harms the style.

Another trick is to enforce a wordcount for a section, and then another one. So take a 500-word piece down to 350, and then down to 250, without losing any meaning.

Using a thesaurus

Those writer's tools I mentioned? A thesaurus and a dictionary: both aimed at finding the right words. The online thesaurus is excellent and on my screen behind *Word* as I type. Yet it can only be used with a dictionary, which I prefer having beside me. The thesaurus offers lists of synonyms that mean exactly or nearly the same as another word or phrase. But check the dictionary for their accuracy — if only "nearly" we'll need to take a view.

And don't go crazy. A thesaurus is at its best when taking a complex word (such as complication) and reducing it to a simple one (such as snag), not the other way around.

Certainly, English — that wonderful combination of Germanic Anglo-Saxon and Romance Norman French — has at least two or often three words for every meaning, uniquely among Indo-European languages. But that's not the 10-15 offered by the thesaurus, which means your choice will need checking for accuracy. Only checking mind. The sound and feel of words are important too, allowing the writer some (though not full) license when varying their language via a thesaurus.

5.   Headlines

Headlines are for articles. Books have a title and sub-title and chapter numbers. True? Not always. In non-fiction, with chapters covering various aspects of multifaceted subjects — rather than simply taking a breather as the plot thickens — some clue regarding a chapter's theme helps commit the reader. And this means that, increasingly, chapters are opting for short headlines to act as descriptors of the material within. All of which makes headlines an area for experimentation, especially for those trying to broaden their audience.

Even if an article meant solely for your peers, why not think of something fun and catchy to describe the range covered by the text below? As with crossheads and numbering, the point is to create a roadmap for your reader with headlines acting as bold road signage: here's what's coming, enjoy!

A good headline can do that as well as intrigue, entice and excite — even (perhaps especially) in books. Some random examples from the shelves behind me:

Chapter Five: **The irresistible lure of the highway** (*Exactly: How Precision Engineers Created the Modern World,* SimonWinchester);

Chapter One: **If You Want to Gather Honey, Don't Kick Over the Beehive** (*How to Win Friends & Influence People,* Dale Carnegie);

Chapter Four: **Cutting a Dash** (*Eats Shoots & Leaves,* Lynne Truss);

Part 5: **Democrats with Cold Feet** (*Russia: A 1000 Year Chronicle of the Wild East,* Martin Sixsmith).

Of course, the vast bulk of non-fiction writing will be for articles, making strong headline-writing a required skill if only to avoid the fate of having a sub-editor write them for you (with the inevitably varying results).

What makes a good headline? Asking a question is certainly one trick and chimes with search engine optimisation needs (see Chapter Five). Questions also help structure articles by setting out, immediately, the proposition or dilemma tackled below. For anyone with an advanced education in the humanities, answering a question is also likely to be their most familiar writing format.

The questions should never be glib. Inquiries such as Why bother? could have your reader asking the same thing. Much better, instead, to inject some jeopardy: Why should we act to save the [insert object in peril], and why now?

Then there's the pun: an addiction of headline writers that rarely results in better headlines. Normally, they involve injecting an inappropriate but associative verb or adjective: *Shipping Company's Profits Sink* kind of thing. Fine, if not so contorted they change expectations of the body copy below.

Certainly, some of the most furious rows I've experienced in publishing have been caused by headline writers being too clever (or not) in trying to generate witty headlines. The worst example, from my own writing, was an article on the English Civil War in which the editor decided the word *civil* could be made into a pun, resulting in a rewrite of the premise and a published article I barely recognised and was ashamed carried my byline — all to serve a pathetic headline pun.

Style consistency is a definite headline requirement. If writing for a publication, check its style: single or double deck, descriptive or enigmatic, use of punctuation, capitalisation etc. But if writing for yourself — perhaps for a blog — you should develop a headline style you like and stick to it. If headlining Chapter One (or blog one etc.) with a question, that should be the style adopted throughout. That said, the same does not apply in reverse: you're allowed to slip in a single question while the other headlines are bold statements.

Capitalisation on headlines is intriguing. UK newspapers tend to avoid the American habit — I assume learnt from the Germans — of capitalising every word other than conjunctions (And I've Even Seen Some Capitalise These). It's a matter of taste and consistency, as ever, though my view is that capitals are for proper nouns and (in contracts only) legal terms. Only those with a plaque on a wall or the side of a ship, or with a birth certificate must be capitalised. Otherwise, use your judgement and be consistent.

Consistency also applies when it comes to length. My long career dealing with financial editorial has resulted in a propensity for the two-deck descriptive headline that can even be read as a standalone summary (read any copy of the *Financial Times* for examples). Yet I find this vaguely unsatisfactory for books and white papers where the aim is not the "quick digest" but the steady absorption of critical (and potentially complex) information.

Certainly, Rule One (or rule one) on headlines is that they're the servant of the body copy not the master. The body copy dictates the headline not the other way around. Puns that can abide by this rule work: Lynne Truss's example above being disappointing in this respect as just two pages of her 35-page *Cutting a Dash* chapter dealt with dashes.

6. Standfirsts

Standfirsts are a common feature of most published articles and sit below (or sometimes above) the headline. They're typographically distinct from both the body copy and the headline and usually include the byline, and their job title, and spend a sentence or two explaining what's to come. They're especially important below non-descriptive catchy-clever headlines that grab our attention but need immediate support regarding the importance of the information below.

Here's where the angle can also receive its first airing, maybe with a hint of the conclusion (or "what's next"), perhaps in the second sentence. It could even be the second airing after a generic headline.

In fact, the headline, standfirst and even the first sentence can all say roughly the same thing, though using different language to say it and with each expanding the information provided. The first sentence of the body copy can help visualise the premise by focusing on a key event — all of which is known as the "inverted pyramid", of which more later.

An invented example:

[Headline] **Did King Harold Live?**

[Standfirst] *"Royal dig" discovers artefacts suggesting monarch es-*

caped 1066 battlefield. The consequences — for historians, for the landowning aristocracy and even for the Royal Family — could be profound, says Oxford University historian Hermione Godwinson

[First sentence] As the light faded on a January afternoon in 2018, Sussex builder and weekend detectorist John Smith — scouring the South Downs for Victorian buttons and Edwardian coins — made a discovery that has opened up perhaps the most critical question in English history.

There's a lot in the above (including some wishful thinking) but the key points are that the reader's attention is drawn through the writing by offering the same poser repeated in different ways, with each offering further information. The standfirst introduces both the author and the angle and — importantly — hints at the reward for the reader should they commit to the article.

The standfirst is the writer's hard-sell. The best (maybe only) chance they'll have to tell the reader that the text below is worth the read. The example above explains the question posed in the headline. Just as often, it's the standfirst posing the question, perhaps making it personal: *So do you need to act?* or *So what do you need to know?* Yet such an obvious read-to-the-end ruse — though now common in the world of click-bait content — can irritate a weary reader, so care is required.

Standfirsts in books or whitepapers? Most commonly not but I've seen them in both.

Last point: by convention both standfirsts and picture captions do not end with a full-stop/period, something sub-editors enjoy pointing out to junior writers.

7. Crossheads

I like crossheads. They're the smaller subheadings that divide chapters or sections or articles, usually every fifth-or-so paragraph and usually in bold type or a slightly larger typeface. Many act as headings for a new section, perhaps lifting a descriptive phrase from the text. Others may be no more than a single word and are there to break up the text — to add white space where there was previously a wall of dense words.

With crossheads, the key is not to waste them. They can be strong signposting for your body copy, helping the reader cut their way through the thicket: "keep going" they're intonating, "this way". Given this, the more generic the crosshead the better — perhaps a four- to five-word summary of the paras ahead, until the next crosshead.

One temptation worth resisting is to theme your crossheads. Waterhouse points out a *News of the World* story on "the most boring man in Britain" with crossheads such as *Waffle, Piffle, Snore,* and *Ho-hum* interspersing the piece. These come across more like an in-joke between sub-editors and are unlikely to encourage readers to continue (quite the opposite, in fact).

Crossheads also do the reader a favour. They allow tired eyes to reach a particular milestone before ending a reading session. Knowing they're not midway through an important point — one they'll have to reread the next time they pick up the book — helps readers unable to complete chapters in a single session (I can find my eyes literally closing after a certain time in the evening). All of which increases reader loyalty.

8. Eyebrows

Eyebrows are the descriptive phrases or words appearing right at the top of the page: any page, online or in print. In books they often repeat the chapter heading while online or within periodicals they tend to assign a broad genre: *Mortgages, Fitness, Bowel Treatment etc*. Eyebrows have become a feature of online content to both catch a reader's eye — nowadays a requirement, thanks to the over-stimulation of modern online publication pages — and as an aid for search-engine optimisation (see Chapter Five).

This is another in the "don't waste them" series of writing elements. For instance, my agency produces lots of content for trade magazines (literally trade — import/export — rather than the generic term for specialist magazines). The eyebrows therefore need to reflect recognisable divisions within that industry while not being so specific they shed potential readers. We often talk of buckets — i.e. broad thematic areas that cover some distinct ground. Examples for trade include *Supply Chains, Regulation, Trade Finance and Digitalisation* — with new ones such as *Sustainability* being added and some, such as *Trade War* (a fear around 2016-18), coming and going.

Many publications use two eyebrows — perhaps the name of the publication or book on the left and the name of the section (or sometimes the author) on the right. And for white papers, they can indicate that they're part of a series with names such as *BankX Insights* or *Market Intelligence* or something similar.

Given this, eyebrows shouldn't be over-thought or overly creative. To invert a genius piece of commercial copywriting, eyebrows should say exactly what they do on the tin.

9.   Quotes

A sprinkling of quotes from luminaries in their field can help enliven any writing, breaking up the body copy while allowing the reader some respite from the author's voice. Quotes are an excellent way of both making and confirming key points. And they show that you've done your research — that your views have depth and gravitas. People of note agree.

But they don't belong everywhere. Opinion pieces for publications can be as short as 600 words (though are usually 800 and above), which affords little room for indulgent quotes from favoured influencers — especially if simply repeating a point. They can also jar: commentaries are usually following a single, narrow, angle by presenting a series of related points. Quotes rarely fit exactly into that premise, although can offer a creative opener or ending.

Too many quotes can leave readers wondering if the author is adding anything of value (other than a dissertation-level collation of contemporary views), a concern compounded when the quotes are so long they interrupt the author's narrative.

Given this, quotes are best when short and integrated into the flow of the article or chapter: no more than two sentences in my view. Certainly, quoting whole passages can start to appear lazy, as if you're allowing others to make your arguments.

Quotes can be presented in three ways:

Integral to your text

Integral quotes can even be within a sentence though they need to be short and could seem so selective they inadvertently distort the meaning or, worse, appear to the reader as a distortion.

Example: While John Smith said "the best beers come from the north" his contemporary, Tom Shepherd, was adamant that the "soil of Kent made for the best hops, and that this Smith fellow can keep his soft Yorkshire water".

As a separate paragraph

Quotes as paras can make the text feel like a novel and are my personal favourite for encouraging reader engagement. They both break up the text — injecting that all-important white space — while maintaining reader fluidity.

Example:

"If a man were called to fix the period in the history of the world during which the condition of the human race was most happy and prosperous he would, without hesitation, name that which elapsed from the death of Domitian to the accession of Commodus," writes D.M. Low in his abridged version of *Gibbon's Decline and Fall of the Roman Empire*. "The vast extent of the Roman empire was governed by absolute power, under the guidance of virtue and wisdom."

By starting a new paragraph with quote marks the text is signalling a new speaker, the identity of whom will remain a mystery until solved, which is best done as soon as possible. I usually inject the author's name after the first punctuation, although the second clause of D.M. Low's opener was so integral to the first it made sense to include it before the name check.

As an entirely separate element on the page

These are usually indented and sometimes in a smaller typeface and can even be in italics. The quote marks are often discarded for such passages and the temptation is to quote significant bodies of text, although this brings up the thorny issue of copyright. At what point does a citation (such as the D.M. Low quote above) infringe copyright?

This is an area requiring more legal expertise than I can offer here, not least because it's also constantly under review. Safe to say that, while my D.M. Low quote is fine — it comes under what the UK's Intellectual

Property Office (IPO) would call "for the purposes of criticism, review or news reporting" — a far longer quote might border on an infringement unless permission is sought and received.

The law was liberalised in 2014, with the IPO stating that: "a short extract from a book in an academic article discussing the book is likely to be permitted, whereas the copying of a long extract from a book, without it being justified by the context, is unlikely to be permitted. You may benefit from this law if you are an author, academic, or even just a casual blogger."

What constitutes a "short extract" is left undefined (I've read mention of 300 words being the convention) as is the fact it's only "likely" to be permitted, meaning that the copyright owners are entitled to contest its use.

Also note: the above applies for work not in the public domain, which — in the US for example — means work first published within the previous 95 years unless published after 1978, for which the protection is 70 years. Though this is applied concurrently with the author's lifespan, meaning that their work is copyright protected for life plus 70 years in the US. The UK remains covered by EU law, which prescribes life plus 70 years for authors and 70 years for published work with no named author.

Finally, with quotes, it's important to cite the reference. While I'm not a big fan of white papers and books so peppered with superscript numbers and footnotes readers become concerned that the author cannot think for themselves, citations for quotes are an exception, not least because the person being cited may demand it.

(more on footnotes in Chapter Six)

10. Lists and bullet points

Lists within the text — perhaps introduced with a colon and separated by commas — are the preference when listing single items. An example is the need for travellers to remember: passports, money, air-tickets and hotel reservations. Why break up the text with such a pathetic list (unless desperate for some white space)? Otherwise, lists are a strong way of supporting an argument while providing the reader with a change of scenery. At this point we are talking, of course, about bullet points, which can:

- provide strong differentiation for points that support the same premise or answer the same question,
- help break up dense blocks of text, injecting the all-important white space, allow for a change of tone, again helping keep the reader awake,
- encourage brevity in the writer, helping them cover lots of ground quickly.

Bullets also:

- usually start with the previous sentence ending in a colon, creating a repeated sentence opening (as with the "Bullets also:" above). Of course, this won't be repeated in the reader's mind each time although the bullet should be written as if it will,
- end in a comma, not a full-stop/period (partly for the reason above), encouraging the reader to trip from one bullet to the next. The bullet acts as the full stop,
- should be numbered only if a specific list of defined elements. If just a series of thoughts, like these, bullets are fine,
- should only be used sparingly. Too many bullets and chapters start resembling *PowerPoint* presentations (which are really an aid for the speaker when addressing an audience, not least because the audience is constantly having to choose between listening to the speaker or reading the bullets), and

- can include an "and" as the penultimate bullet's ending, which will encourage a reader perhaps tiring of bullets to keep going.

Of course, there are other elements to a writing project: the chapters themselves, as well as graphs, tables, images, forewords and appendices (all dealt with in Chapter Six). But the above ten items constitute the kit required for the most critical part of our writing project: producing the first draft.

Once we have a first draft we have a book — or an article or a white paper — so it's time to get on with it. After all, that book won't write itself.

Chapter Four

Writing by numbers (or producing first drafts)

Let's write that first draft by constructing a piece of writing by numbers, although the visualisation should be less an outlined picture with numbers in shapes ready for our paint and more an IKEA flatpack or Jamie Oliver recipe (future readers may question what these are, providing an immediate lesson regarding the currency of any analogy). In fact, given that we're building something vertical, the best analogy from here-on will be the building of a skyscraper.

Step One: Confirm the angle

Yes, we've tackled this previously, but we must now apply it. Does our angle stack up, providing the required central core for our writing project? Is it strong enough for everything to hang off? Of course, articles can generally sustain a single angle. Books, however, will need something sustainable over hundreds of pages, requiring it to be broken down into manageable sub-themes.

Certainly, a book must have a central theme — such as how professionals can write better non-fiction — with each chapter or section (if a white paper) having its own ancillary angle. Yet each must be a supportive part of the whole.

For instance, a book chronicling the disruption caused to the modern publishing industry by digitalisation (the over-arching theme, though still one pursing a particular angle) will need a series of chapters looking at various aspects, each with their own complementary angle. How the internet blew up print magazines' business models, for instance, and how the book industry was slow to exploit digital forms of publishing. The decline of the independent bookseller as part of the internet's impact on high streets provides a further angle as does the growth of self-publishing.

The point is that each provides further evidence supporting the central theme. If they don't, either they shouldn't be in the book or you're writing the wrong book.

With the angle decided for each chapter — and perhaps written at the top of the page as a first-draft headline (to be amended later) — we must ensure it runs through every paragraph and even every sentence. I write a paragraph and then reread it asking myself "does this support the angle?" Directly, not tangentially. There's no meandering, no interesting asides, no indulgent anecdotes (they can be added later if required). This is the concrete core of the skyscraper. The central lift/elevator shaft from which everything hangs.

Step Two: Format the page

Most books are written using Microsoft *Word*, which is annoying software when it comes to formatting. Yet it's worth persevering because the right formatting encourages better writing. When starting as a full-time journalist in the early 1990s the wizened editors I feared most had spent their careers writing for the hot-metal typesetting process, which meant they insisted on "galley proofs" for copy submissions.

In some cases their draft articles were printed on paper about half the width of an A4 page. And while that now seems quaint the habit of typing copy in columns similar in width to those likely to appear on the page is a good one. Too often I'm sent drafts from juniors who've battled away writing articles across the full width of an A4 page. I send them back, asking the writer to format the article correctly as well as undertake the inevitable edits required once they start writing in columns mirroring the final published page.

Writing is visual. The look of the page matters. Just as an artist paints to suit the size of the canvas so a writer should tailor their writing to the format of the published page.

What's the correct format? There isn't one: web-content, books, magazines and blogs all follow their own styles. But the ageing hacks that first taught me instilled within me a formatting discipline for newspapers and magazines that also seems to work for books, so that's the one I pass on to trainees. And it does seem to improve their writing.

Here are the key points:

- Using *Word*, write in a single column with the column-width no more than 11 centimetres. This mirrors the likely column-width on the printed page (in fact, is somewhat generous) and offers a wide right-hand margin for hand-written edits,

- Ensure the Ruler is visible (under View in the top menu), and use that to indent the first line of each para to one centimetre. Never use the tab to do this as the typesetter will have to go through your entire draft removing the tabs (and irritating typesetters is an own-goal worth avoiding),

- Choose a plain typeface that doesn't distract. I'm typing on *Calibri* (Body), size 11, although I'm equally happy with *Arial*. *Serif* typefaces are also fine — such as *Times New Roman* — and are likely to be the typeface used by the publishers. While books tend to use *serif*, I prefer *sans-serif* (without the end-strokes, for instance, on the T, N and R of *Times New Roman*) when drafting: plain and simple, so good for spotting typos,

- I choose a line-spacing (or "leading") of 1.15 because it mirrors the likely look on the published page although sometimes ask juniors to go to 1.5 — again to allow hand-written edits if required,

- Align text to the left margin ("range left"). Justified text (though often used in publications) makes spacing errors harder to spot.

That's it: simple stuff but in my view transformative in readying us for the writing task ahead. Of course, *Word* has an annoying habit of trying to predict your formatting choices, especially after a change of formatting such as a series of bullets. But it's worth the battle — formatting matters.

Step Three: Write block one, and two

We now have the central core of our skyscraper. From our content research, we also have a sketch of the likely elements or points to be covered within a chapter. These are the sections of the skyscraper that will, when applied, hang from the core. They're our blocks of writing and can be tackled in any order, and later added to the whole structure in our chosen sequence.

So let's write block one of that content without worrying whether it's block one in our sketched structure. It doesn't matter. At this stage, we might not even have a complete picture of all the blocks required. Indeed, some will occur to us as we write. Others can end up being two blocks once we fully consider what's involved. Some can even be discarded.

We just need to start writing, so let's write what's at the front of our mind at that moment. For instance, if our *digital disruption of publishing* angle above was a single chapter — perhaps for a book with an overall angle of how technology has transformed all of the media industry — the blocks would potentially cover magazines, ebooks, *Amazon* etc. Each requires just a few paras. So while we need to be succinct, we can write them in any order.

Perhaps the magazine industry is upper-most in our mind. Fine, let's write that bit first. Just bang it out (applying the correct formatting, of course) — a stream-of-conscious diatribe onto the page, perhaps 350 words (if an article) or 600 if part of a book. Done.

We now have a first draft of block one. If each article or chapter has five blocks, we've just drafted 20% of Chapter One. We should immediately reread our writing, now thinking about the angle. Have we stuck to the premise posed by the angle, in this case the internet's disruption of the magazine industry's business model? If not, reshape the text to do so, perhaps by adding or rewriting an opening sentence to ensure it reads as if a run-on from the angle (similar in feel to the bullets running on from the colon).

How many paras? Four or five? Fine. Are they in the right order? One trick is to try putting your last para first. Perhaps you were building your argument, making the last para the most relevant. If so, put that top with the others adding justification and context.

And has every sentence been checked for unnecessary adjectives, hyperbole, pleonasms and tautologies? Try inverting one sentence per para, maybe starting with the object or the verb. And try starting the last sentence with "and" (cheap tricks, I realise, but they can improve the flow of the block).

Step Four: Write the tougher blocks

We can repeat the above for all the blocks, tackling them in the order we mentally feel ready for them rather than as they appear in the structure (though we should check that the order is correct). Writing the most obvious or easiest blocks first will build our confidence, helping us tackle the harder ones once in our stride.

But what of the really hard blocks — where we are under-confident of the material or worry about our knowledge or its relevance to the angle? Here we should not jump straight into stream-of-consciousness writing but instead write a series of bullet points. Bullets mean we're focused entirely on the points being made — the content — not on sentence construction.

Once we have six to ten bullets, each making a different point, and we consider (on rereading) that they're all relevant, we can think about their order. While keeping them as bullets, try different permutations to decide which work best. Then remove the bullets.

Now we can worry about sentence construction, including sense, tense and flow. It should also adhere to the angle, with each para a run-on from that central premise. And we need to decide whether each point should be its own paragraph or whether some can be conflated together. Again, tight language matters, even at this stage.

This is such a tried-and-tested formula for writing with my team of writers we often apply it to entire articles or parts of a white paper. And we insist on it for trainees and under-confident writers (perhaps employed for alternative skills), especially when dealing with new subjects.

For an entire article (say 1500 words) we ask for 20 or so bullets, all separate stand-alone points but all relevant. The reason for doing so is simple: the writer is separating the content from the writing and ensuring that, first, they have the right content. Remember the process: angle, content, structure, style. So, once happy that each bullet is relevant we then need to order them — perhaps first dividing the 20 or so into blocks of four to six before ordering the blocks and removing the bullets.

The 20-bullets route for developing content is such a strong process for converting difficult or technical content into coherent passages that I still regularly resort to it, especially when dealing with new material. And even when I feel confident enough to bang out the paras, it's always mentally in the background when I write, like some imaginary scaffolding.

Step Five: Stitch the blocks together

By now we should have five or six blocks of writing, each around four to five paragraphs, all well-written and all conforming to the angle for that chapter (which conforms to the central theme of the writing project).

Now we build the skyscraper: block by block. It's not the roof or the entrance — it's the bulk of the building. It's what makes it a skyscraper.

First, we need to decide on the order. Was our initial structure right or has the writing process changed our view? If written as separate *Word* files it might even be worth printing them out and reviewing them separately. In what order should they be presented? The printouts allow for some shuffling before combining them on a single *Word* file for that chapter or article.

Don't worry about the opening or the conclusion: they're to come, as are the headline and standfirst.

Two things matter now:

Separate the blocks with crossheads

As stated, crossheads can be a single word or phrase and can also be numbered if your project allows (often the norm for white papers and academic articles). Put crossheads in bold and/or italics. But remember they're not headlines. They simply divide the blocks and offer some signposting for the reader.

Stitch the blocks together

I use a method for this that sometimes attracts criticism, especially from trained journalists. I add "link words" to the beginnings of sections and also to the paragraphs. The aim is to encourage the text to flow and for each paragraph to be read as part of the whole. Para by para, the aim is to support the angle, which link words can do.

The following link words can be used:

i. **If the next para supports the previous one (building the case):** *Additionally, Also, Furthermore, What's more, Certainly,*

ii. **If the next para offers a qualifying but relevant point:** *However, That said, Alternatively,*

This is a controversial short-cut that achieves two things. First, it ensures that the text reads as a coherent whole and encourages the reader to treat it as such. Second, it allows the author to develop their voice, something we'll come back to in Chapter Five.

Importantly, the final edit will remove as many of these link words as possible, perhaps rewriting the sentences to make the link implicit. The link words are for the first draft, allowing us the comfort of seeing that the text and, importantly, the structure works. That said, while temporary stitching, some (a minority) may survive the final edit.

Hate this idea? You're not alone. Try Ann Handley's alternative in *Everybody Writes*. She asks us to "draw natural connections between paragraphs". Pick an idea from the previous para and connect it to an idea in the next as I did with this para's opening question. Both achieve the same — text that flows and feels correctly ordered.

Step Six: Add an opening paragraph

Now we can "top and tail" our work, first focusing on the opening paragraph. For articles, this is where the "inverted pyramid" is applied although I also think it works well for most (though not all) chapters. The inverted pyramid is a journalism-school technique for newspaper articles stating that the core message of the piece under consideration should be captured in the first sentence or two or in the first para.

For articles, this could well be a repeat of the angle (from the headline and/or standfirst) as shown in the King Harold example in Chapter Three. For books, it can do the same by linking to the previous chapter, even if only to remind the reader that we're on a journey and have reached a certain point.

"Having explored [X] we now turn our attention to [Y]."

That said, we need to explain Y upfront. Do not force the reader to discover Y through their own painful evaluation of your tangled suppositions throughout the paras below. State it: this is what is meant by Y, here's how it fits with the angle and here's what's coming — all in the opening para.

Some white papers even open new sections with bullet point summaries of the text below, a practical if unromantic reminder that the reader's time is precious and their attention an ephemeral commodity. Personally, I think the job can be done through a strong opening paragraph that also trips them into the second paragraph, and the third... all helped by strong signposting via crossheads and the judicial use of link words.

The inverted pyramid creates an easily understandable structure and process for our chapter construction. It starts with the core message captured as succinctly as possible. This is followed by supporting point one, supporting point two and so on — all hanging from the core angle. Of course, the supporting points are the blocks, divided by the crossheads. These now hang from the top in the order that makes the strongest points first.

It's a simple technique that gets the job done. Yet some writers will reject the inverted pyramid on principle, thinking that books, in particular, need chapters to build rather than have the point thrown in the reader's face immediately, weakening their commitment to the whole. I disagree. Their commitment will be all the stronger for having a clear notion of what's ahead, with the text offering detail, justification and examples.

But for those that feel it intuitively wrong, I offer another tip. Too often writers start any piece too far from their core subject — as if they're limbering up with some general points or coming from a tangential angle to tweak the reader's curiosity. I notice it most when writers are approaching a new subject. So try removing the first sentence. Does the piece still make sense without it? If yes, try the second sentence. And maybe even the entire first paragraph.

Certainly, it's surprising how often this works. And how it improves the overall piece in doing so. Another way of looking at the same conundrum is by asking the question, "should this be where this chapter starts?" If the answer is anything other than a resounding "yes" the answer is almost certainly "no" and it's writer's vanity preventing us from realising it.

Whatever your method, a strong opening para is vital. Some even put it in bold or a different type to give it emphasis: all to help win the reader's commitment. I'd rather just make it a belter of a para that begins with an unforgettable opening sentence. All the more so when it's Chapter One.

Let's wander into fiction for a brief moment just to remind ourselves of some of the most unforgettable first lines ever written and what makes them so memorable.

> "It's a truth universally acknowledged, that a single man in possession of a good fortune, must be in want of a wife," Jane Austen, *Pride & Prejudice*.

Probably the most pitch-perfect inverted pyramid ever written.

> "It was the best of times, it was the worst of times, it was the age of wisdom, it was the age of foolishness, it was the epoch of belief, it was the epoch of incredulity, it was the season of Light, it was the season of Darkness, it was the spring of hope, it was the winter of despair, we had everything before us, we had nothing before us, we were all going direct to heaven, we were all going direct the other way," Charles Dickens, *A Tale of Two Cities*.

More an opening para, and it could have done with an edit, but Dickens by 1859 was at the top of his game and was clearly excited by the subject in front of him: the French Revolution. I suspect he bounced around the house repeating this to anyone who'd listen after penning such an exciting opener. Epoch-changing adventure awaits.

> "We were somewhere around Barstow on the edge of the desert when the drugs began to take hold," Hunter S. Thompson, *Fear and Loathing in Las Vegas*.

More mind-bending than epoch-changing but a cliff-hanger of a first sentence. There's also the intrigue offered by seemingly insignificant detail.

> "No one would have believed in the last years of the nineteenth century that this world was being watched keenly and closely by intelligences greater than man's and yet as mortal as his own; that as men busied themselves about their various concerns they were scrutinised and studied, perhaps almost as narrowly as a man with a microscope might scrutinise the transient creatures that swarm and multiply in a drop of water," H.G. Wells, *The War of the Worlds*.

Almost impossible to read without adopting Richard Burton's gravelly voice and having Jeff Wayne's music crashing into your consciousness. But that simply underlines its utter, overwhelming, terror.

> "If you really want to hear about it, the first thing you'll probably want to know is where I was born, and what my lousy childhood was like, and how my parents were occupied and all before they had me, and all that David Copperfield kind of crap, but I don't feel like going into it, if you want to know the truth," J.D. Salinger, *The Catcher in the Rye*.

Enigmatic rather than illuminating but the reader is immediately struck by the coarse language and the fact the narrator is clearly troubled and has attitude.

Anyone thinking these authors sat down to write their books and the first thing they wrote were these great openers has a lot to learn about the writing process. My guess is they were at least halfway through — utterly absorbed in their material — when these openings hit them out of the blue, maybe when occupied elsewhere. In each case, they'd have scrambled in a panic to find a notebook to capture the words before they left their heads forever. And, in each case, we owe that handy notebook a huge debt.

Step Seven: Add an ending

Do we need a conclusion? Not if we follow the inverted pyramid method to the letter. The aim here is to be able to cut articles to length from the bottom up. And while this is the sign of a well-trained journalist it leaves no room for a conclusion, which — given the inverted pyramid — should have been at the top anyhow.

Yet this can seem unsatisfactory for long-form writing projects where we need periodic signposting indicating that "this is the ground so far covered, and on we go".

Conclusions should never look entirely bolted-on (though they will be). Nor should they simply repeat the opening, all of which can start sounding restrictive until we realise that these very restrictions are pointing the way. In fact, that's exactly what we do: we point the way. What's coming next and, importantly — given what we've just read — why what's coming next is not only critical but the obvious follow on.

Of course, this has the added satisfaction of being another check on our structure. Is what's coming next the obvious follow-on? If not, we might need to rethink or at least be clear in our signalling that we're taking a diversion.

Chapter and section endings can provide emphatic signposting for the reader or they can tease — offering a veiled hint of the tremendous insight ahead. If the project is solving a mystery now's the time for a riddle to keep them hanging on for the revelation, which is just a little later on.

"If [X] showed us how things are, could [Y] reveal how things might be in the future?

Obviously, standalone commentary articles cannot rely on such segues, although can follow a purist's version of the inverted pyramid by simply ending when the points are made. Yet many will think this too stark, especially for opinion pieces crying out for something conclusive as a sign-off. So why not also adopt the XY approach — with Y the inevitable intangible hypothesis?

"If we ignore these warning signs [X], the future [Y] could be a lot worse than we think."

A final trick for articles is to end where we began. Not by repeating the point but by returning to a visual hook that formed our opening. Did our opening paragraph begin at a particular place, perhaps describing a child waiting in a hospital or a festival street scene or by citing a particular law or regulation — or maybe with a quotation from a respected source? This adds visual imagery to the narrative and provides a suitable ending: little Lara being wheeled into the operating theatre or the street cleaners moving in as the festival ends, or by outlining what's next for that law's passage onto the statute books. We're back where we started, though the story has moved on.

(more on segues in Chapter Five)

Step Eight: Add the headline

We've already discussed headlines, but we now have to write one. A good percentage of articles submitted to me for approval have no headline. When I ask why, the answer usually revolves around the writer's inability to think of one. "Nothing at all came to you?" I ask, "well, nothing that was any good" comes the usual reply.

If they cannot think of a good headline, I advise them to think of a bad one. And then keep thinking.

Agonising over headlines while assuming they have to be brilliant is a common error. Certainly, writers tend to overthink headlines, which is unsurprising given the great tradition of headline writing in the Anglosphere — summing up some of the most critical moments in recent history (and admittedly some less critical ones).

Ford to City: Drop Dead (*Daily News* on New York's failed plea to the president for a bailout in 1975).

Crisis What Crisis? (*The Sun* sealing PM Jim Callaghan's fate during the Winter of Discontent 1979).

Gotcha (*The Sun* on the sinking of the *General Belgrano* in 1982).

Freddie Starr Ate My Hamster (*The Sun*, again, in 1986).

Up Yours Delors (*The Sun*, of course — this time offering its opinion on monetary union 1990).

Notice something? The most memorable headlines conform to the inverted-pyramid structure of news writing in that they encapsulate the story. This even applies to what is widely considered the greatest headline in American newspaper history:

Headless Body Found in Topless Bar (*New York Post*, 1983).

Sure, some need further explanation (and the *Gotcha* headline seemed distasteful, even at the time). But the assumed obsession of both writers and sub-editors to invent witty or punning headlines — or to sensationalise — is misplaced. It's that critical encapsulation that matters.

Keith Waterhouse (of newspaper style fame) talks of headlines becoming so important to tabloid journalism that they can become completely divorced from the stories beneath them: *Up Yours!* being cited as an example. No, not *The Sun* to Jacques Delors, but the *Daily Mirror's* headline for a story concerning England cricketer Graham Gooch's contract negotiations for a controversial tour. Gooch's only quotes: that he's yet to receive a contract from the selectors and that, when he does, he'll sign it no matter where the destination.

"Who exclaimed 'Up yours!' and to whom, remains a mystery," mused Waterhouse.

I like headline writing, going back to my days page-editing the youth element of *The Independent* (called *The Indy*). Given the readership, we thought the cornier the pun the better: *Seacat Trials Throw up New Problems* being one of my favourites (about a new class of high-speed ferries that to this day are famous for inducing seasickness).

But I've got over the obsession since. And I sympathise — headline writing can seem daunting to the uninitiated.

Some tips:

- Write that bad headline (maybe explaining the angle in one sentence) and reread it aloud, perhaps repeating it in different word orders. Listen out for the smoothest-sounding combination. This is no time for a reader snag so settle on something that sounds pleasing and easily understandable,

- If you've followed the inverted pyramid, read the first sentence and see if it can be shortened. For practice try it on some famous book openings: *Men Get Rich and Then go Wife Hunting, Claims Jane Austen,* which is probably more suited to Waterhouse's tabloids than the world of professional writing (*Young men acquire wealth prior to seeking a life partner, opines highly regarded Bath novelist*),

- Try telling someone what your piece is about. And then try doing so again in under ten words,

- Try writing it in one sentence before applying Zinsser's brackets to any superfluous elements. And then try inverting the sentence, putting the object or verb first,
- Reread the piece and jot down the keywords, also looking at the crossheads for inspiration,
- If that doesn't work, put the keywords into an online thesaurus, looking for the shortest versions,
- If desperate for something pithy, think of a cultural reference that might work. My favourite: *Revenge of the Nerds*, for an article I wrote on how over-collateralised securitisation caused the 2008 crash (subsequently "stolen" by *The Economist* and many other publications).

Otherwise, and as stated previously, headlines should follow a consistent style if using them for chapter headings in a book or for the title of white papers that may form a series. This includes headline foibles such as the use of punctuation (fine, if used sparingly) and the craziness of headline capitalisation (not fine, but follow any style set by the publisher). It also means using active verbs (*College Opens New Building*) and the present tense rather than passive verbs (*New Building Opened by College*) and the past tense.

Step Nine: Add the standfirsts, bylines and picture captions

As stated, standfirsts sell the writing below, enticing the reader across the threshold by offering the promise within. Non-fiction books are often read piecemeal, perhaps using the table of contents or index to navigate required reading. Meanwhile magazines are flicked through for items that grab the attention, while online articles don't even have that luxury. We're lucky the reader's opened the page and keeping them there will be hard work. And it's usually the standfirst at the top of the article or chapter doing the hardest work.

Given this, the best standfirsts:

- inject some jeopardy: perhaps a question or a relevant proposition added as a twist (*But is the market overheating?*) — though make sure the text addresses this,
- keep your audience in mind. Who must read your piece? Address them directly (*Here's what first-time-buyers need to know*),
- justify your article. Like a college tutorial in which you must "defend your thesis" here's your chance to sum-up your angle favourably and to even undermine what's gone before (*Previous studies have asked the wrong questions and got the wrong answers. Here we ask the right questions*).

As for adding standfirsts at the top of the chapter, it's your call but something that leads the reader down the page is worth experimenting with. We've mentioned bullets (which I dislike as a crime against the body copy) and the notion of putting the first para in bold or larger type. So why not see if standfirsts work?

Bylines

If you're writing an article or contributing a chapter to an edited book on a particular subject (sometimes called an anthology) now's the time to add a byline. We'll deal with your full biography in Chapter Six. Our concern here is that your byline, which often forms part of the standfirst, justifies you as the writer of the text below.

Unfortunately, who's writing a piece is as important — if not more so — than what's being written. And while this can be frustrating, amateurs needn't despair. It just needs a little tinkering in order to present yourself well on the page.

In PR this is known as the "between-the-commas" description: the statement after a name of a person or institution that defines them and their expertise. My advice here is to always provide one as, otherwise, the editor will have to (and you might dislike what they invent).

And that this is no time for modesty. Of course, your job title may feel inadequate or irrelevant, which is why the between-the-commas description needs to do some work, perhaps focusing on your experience.

An example for a book on ceramics:

"Deborah Wedgewood, Director of Art at the Museum of Littletown [relevant but not important] and a specialist in 18th-Century ceramics [relevant and important]"

Yet what if Deborah works as a solicitor, making her job title entirely irrelevant? Then just extrapolate the expertise:

"Deborah Wedgewood, an authority and published author on 18th-Century ceramics"

The above statement is true even if she'll only be "published" once this book is out. And, these days, blogs on *LinkedIn* can count as published (though we should replace "author" with "writer"). As stated, this is no time to be coy.

Also, never use the word "amateur". There's no such concept in publishing. If you're writing on a subject and seeking publication then you're not a passive onlooker or hobbyist. You're an actively engaged participant seeking recognition.

An example of this is my late father. An engineer by training, his leisure-time obsession was the English Civil War. He was particularly fascinated by the Civil War defences of London, which he investigated for years — dragging me on walks along their course and recording their impact on modern street names and even the landscaping in places such as Hyde Park. He wrote one article on the subject for a re-enactment society newsletter run by a friend, which led to an invitation to contribute a chapter for a weighty book, *London and the Civil War* edited by Stephen Porter, the

Royal Commissioner on the Historical Monuments of England.

Of course, this triggered serious doubts in my unqualified dad who became concerned that, as an engineer with a hobby, his thesis would be dismissed. Yet the between-the-commas introduction, I assume written by Stephen, dispelled any concerns from naysayers by turning his amateurism on its head.

> "Peter Kelsey, a Chartered Structural Engineer whose principal field of activity is forensic work"

Try arguing with him over Civil War defences after that description! His biography also mentioned his one previous article for his friend's newsletter. So there he stood, alongside royal commissioners and professors and noted historians: all thanks to the word *forensic*. He was proud as punch.

Picture captions

Studies have shown that headlines or standfirsts are not the first elements of any newspaper article read by the reader. It's the caption under the photograph or image. We'll deal with the images later. Our concern here is the caption because they're clearly too important to be left to the page-editor.

As well as explaining the image, captions should intrigue — offering a nugget of the treasures within the text. If it's an image of a person or building we should offer more than their names and/or titles, perhaps even injecting some controversy.

> "Marie Curie: The Polish-born physicist and chemist who conducted pioneering research into radioactivity. Despite being the only Nobel Prize winner in two fields she constantly struggled for resources and recognition because of her gender"

Another example:

"Immortalised by Charles Dickens as the home of Little Nell, The Old Curiosity Shop in London spent many years as a dairy on an estate gifted by Charles II to one of his mistresses"

And if not given the luxury of such lengthy wordcounts, we need to work even harder to intrigue the reader.

"Marie Curie: the Nobel Prize-winning physicist who battled sexism"

"The Old Curiosity Shop: Little Nell's home and the Merry Monarch's immoral gift"

HEADLINE				
Standfirst				
Inverted pyramid opening para				
Section 1				
Crosshead 1				
Section 2				
Crosshead 2				
Section 3				
What's next				

(The ANGLE)

Step Ten: Check your facts

We now have a complete first draft (congratulations by the way), making this the beginning of the editing process. And job Number One is to check our facts. If delayed until later — after styling or further edits or after being laid out on the page, perhaps with supporting graphs — those pesky errors hiding within our text will become entrenched: gaining an inertia that, unless there's a deliberate process for checking and removing them, will be there on publication.

So, with the metaphorical ink not yet dry we have the perfect opportunity to ensure the accuracy of our material. The closer we get to publication — with dodgy facts embedded within — the more painful the amendments and the more reluctant we'll be to remove them. Think of factual errors like a disease. Spotted early, they can be dealt with efficiently. Spotted late, and any cure is both painful and potentially fatal for the project.

Think I exaggerate? Literary history is littered with discarded books due to factual errors, a recent and notorious example being feminist Naomi Wolf's 2019 book *Outrages*. A major plank of the book dealt with the persecution and execution of homosexuals in Victorian Britain. A worthy subject, yet Wolf misread the (admittedly confusing) court documents of the time, claiming those that had served custodial sentences had actually been executed. Also, many she claimed had been convicted of consensual adult "sodomy" had in fact been child rapists.

Confronted live on radio about her mistakes, Wolf acknowledged the execution error, resulting in the first edition being pulped. Yet she dug in with the other assertions despite historians presenting written evidence to back their claims. In the eyes of many the book became fatally undermined despite its highly supportable overall angle, and Wolf's reputation was harmed. All of which could have been avoided with some strong early-stage fact-checking.

So what should we check? Obviously, all facts and figures, but what else?

Check names

Check spellings every time names appear. Don't become comfortable because you got them right first time. Many first names can be spelt differently: Marc/Mark, Stephen/Steven, Sean/Shaun Jane/Jayne Anne/Ann, and there are about 14 ways of spelling Mohammed. Surnames also have many confusing near-versions: Johnson/Johnstone, Goleman/Goldman Davies/Davis etc.

Of all the errors that can make it right through the editing process, misspelt names are both the most common and the most embarrassing, as well as the least forgiven by those being wronged. And, yes, I did carefully check the spelling of Mihály Csíkszentmihályi, mentioned in Chapter Two.

Check dates

As you might have guessed by now, my favourite non-fiction genre — at least as a reader — is history, where the dates are central to the narrative. Yet chronology is vital for so many areas — scientific research, law and financial markets, to name just three — that we should double-check every date. The year a report was published or law enacted or a disaster struck matters because its causes will have been events that happened before it and its consequences those that followed. Confuse the order and your essential narrative becomes undermined.

Check quotes

At my PR firm, some of our biggest fights with publications come from real or perceived misquotes. The issues fall into two buckets. First, our clients can claim they didn't say something that's been attributed to them.

Second, they can claim the journalist has taken them out of context.

The first is easily — though often awkwardly — dealt with because we do our best to record all interviews. I also have a former journalist's habit of taking very extensive notes from every conversation. This has not always worked in my favour, for instance when having to tell a client that, yes, they did actually say that. Nonetheless, if using interviews as source material, ensure they're recorded.

And it's polite to seek approval for any quotes being used. Many journalists — for instance on the *The Wall Street Journal* — refuse to check quotes, which is fine for a big, bad global newspaper such as *"The Journal"*. But not so fine for you: interviewees are entitled to check what appears as a direct quote from them. That said, it can be irritating when an interviewee — on seeing their words in print — suddenly wants to qualify their statements or even withdraw them altogether. An occupational hazard I'm afraid.

While a bigger subject than the afforded space here, your interviewees should understand that they are "on the record" when being interviewed (meaning you intend using what they say and attributing it to them, which *The Journal* — to be fair — makes clear before any interview). Of course, interviewees should go "off the record" for anything they say that they wouldn't want attributed to them by name (convention suggesting they should do so before saying it).

As a writer, you can save yourself some time by predicting what will likely cause an interviewee concern in print — asking if they'd like that "off the record". You can then quote them as *an industry expert*, which often works well on the page (adding an air of mystery and subterfuge) though you'll be surprised by the number of times they'll reply "no, I'm happy to be quoted on this" (though they'll appreciate being asked), which can also be taken as a vote of confidence in you as a writer.

Yet this opens up the trickier notion of context. Being quoted "out of context" can infuriate interviewees so it might be worth outlining the context when quote checking (if uncertain, I sometimes send the prior para with the quote). Your writing project has an angle and you might be interviewing people who'd pursue a different angle if writing on the same subject. Given this, you should not feel compelled to confess the entire angle when checking a quote for one chapter/section of your work — just the context of the quote will suffice.

That said, if your interviewee is central to your premise — with their quotes likely to pepper your work — they deserve the courtesy of knowing whether you're onside with their views or seeking to oppose them. "Hit-job journalism" in which the interviewer poses as an ally while lulling the interviewee into a false sense of security to "expose" them in print is best left to the dark arts of Fleet Street journalism. Here, it's just as likely to undermine you as it is to betray your target.

Check your prejudices

Another dilemma concerns bias. Some of the most convincing articles or books I've ever read are those that — rather than stating an angle or premise and seeking to justify it by adding facts — seek to test it by presenting every counter-argument possible. This immediately refutes any accusations of confirmation bias in your content. It also concurs with one of my favourite philosophers on what's known as falsifiability. In demarcating science from non-science, said Karl Popper, science (which we can extend to anything factually based) relies on the hypothesis (our angle) being tested by it being conceivably proven false.

Therefore, if we're putting forward an argument we should present not simply what supports that argument but also what could undermine it. For instance, going back to our example book in Step One — about the digital challenges to publishing — we'll need to ensure we don't undermine our angle by ignoring strong counter-arguments such as the growing sales of audio books and the resilience of local booksellers able to turn themselves into community hubs. These test the hypothesis and will need to be absorbed into the debate rather than discarded as inconvenient asides.

Another helpful philosophical notion is G.W.F. Hegel's idea of presenting a thesis and an antithesis in order to arrive at a synthesis. If we present arguments in this way — as legitimate arguments and counter-arguments and with your view as the synthesis between them — they'll be accepted as far more credible than an unbalanced account that ignores awkward information.

Peer-reviewed articles

Finally, with respect to fact-checking, there are peer-reviewed articles, often targeting the official journals of professional bodies and a common way for practitioners to make their name. The most common issues that come back from the peer reviewers include missing references, a lack of technical clarifications, "non-conventional data presentation" (perhaps from an unrecognised source) and the use of confusing or ambiguous phraseology. All but the last element (which we'll deal with in the next chapter) demonstrates why preparing for peer review belongs here rather than under style.

This is a specialist area with its own conventions, often unique to a particular occupation. And while my PR firm has ghost-written for many such journals, especially for professionals using English as their second language, our recommendation is that writers work with the editor on preparing work for publication. They will all have publicly available guidelines helping writers prepare manuscripts and are usually very approachable: their job is, after all, to encourage submissions that are worthy of publication.

Chapter Five

Views on style

1. Developing your voice

Authenticity is vital for non-fiction. There's none of the suspended disbelief of fiction. Your work should reek of you. Acquaintances reading my books often say they cannot remove my voice, which they report as a problem but I take as a compliment, though it did me no favours with my first published book.

That book was meant to humorously evidence my calamitous attempts at learning the arts of the lothario. But to be accepted within the "lad-lit" genre (popular in the late 1990s) I assumed my character needed to show more confidence than the angst-ridden fumbling idiot that was the real me. So the book, while successfully adopting my voice, documented attitudes that were not mine and that appear insensitive to contemporary readers.

Thankfully, I learnt the lessons and, for my later books, developed a voice that was both genuinely mine and reflected my true values. And notice we're talking about "developing" our voice, not finding it. It will differ from our spoken voice, though still needs to be authentically ours.

I'm often accused of being too passionate in conversation. Too intense and emotional. And while this makes me hard work as a dinner-party guest — not least because I can become too readily combative and defensive — it adds lucidity to my writing and generates, I hope, that all-important but fleetingly acquired need for any writer: reader buy-in.

We can think of our writing voice as our preferred persona. Our best self. It's what we wish we'd said at that dinner party: perfected and then beautifully delivered — something we failed to do at the time thanks to being emotionally triggered by someone more confident or on top of the detail. Yet it must still be us. Just the best us. The edited us.

Warm-up required

Chances are your written voice has yet to settle and might not fully until you're well into your writing stride. Every book I've written has required a rewrite of the first (and sometimes second and third) chapter once my rhythm and style has settled. As with most pursuits, we need to "warm up", hence why we've come this far — with a fully written first draft — before tackling style.

"Perhaps your style won't solidify for years as your style, your voice," says Zinsser, who is the leading authority on finding your voice (and much else besides). "Just as it takes time to find yourself as a person, it takes time to find yourself as a stylist, and even then your style will change as you grow older."

His view (and mine): be yourself when you write. He talks of college students writing as if they were "desiccated alumni 30 years out" assuming their work won't be taken seriously otherwise. Indeed, there might be those in "the academy" (by which I mean any organisation with intellectual gatekeepers holding your fate in their hands) that expect work to be presented in a certain way, usually via a high scholarly tone. But that doesn't mean you should acquiesce. Or at least acquiesce fully.

Again, the restrictions could work in your favour — providing a framework within which you weave your personality. Anyway, for any ambitious writer, academics should be but a tiny part of their targeted audience, however important those crusty old pedagogues think themselves.

But Zinsser's point is critical. Never write as someone you're not. While the written word will always be more ordered than conversation — and rightly so — we shouldn't adopt words and phrases we'd not use in discussion with, say, a peer professional (and even that's a high bar: an intelligent layperson is perhaps a better benchmark). Sounding off with the pomposity of a lawyer in Dickensian London, when we're a post-graduate student with a thesis to write, not only opens us up to ridicule, it almost certainly harms our writing.

Zinsser talks about using words such as *indeed* and *moreover* that we'd never use in conversation. I'm more forgiving, given their usefulness as link words if used sparingly. His essential point is that the vocabulary we choose should be genuinely ours. So even as we tighten the language used in the first draft — now making it as taut and compelling as we can — we should use phrases and words that still chime with our genuine voice.

For instance, I tend to caveat statements with the word *perhaps* (from a quick search, 43 times in the first draft of chapters one to four). Type perhaps into the online thesaurus and I'm offered *perchance*, which is an unlikely word to hear from me (more the Dickensian lawyer). But I'm also offered *maybe*, which is more my style. So I've just doubled my options without losing my voice.

Retaining our voice

While words are important, rhythm and cadence are vital. If we speak with the poetic lilt of a Welsh bard, that's what readers will expect to hear in our writing (and is often why Welsh politicians — from Lloyd George to Nye Bevan to Neil Kinnock — are credited with strong oratory skills). It's probably our greatest asset as a writer so to drown it in grammatical strictures, qualified language and overly cautious or overblown corporate doublespeak — what Kingsley Amis in *The King's English* calls "committee English" — is a self-defeating tragedy.

Yet good writing is not simply a question of retaining our relaxed verbal intonation despite its obvious authenticity. It requires improvement — sharpening — to ensure it's the best rendition of us. Message rich and compelling, as well as an easy read.

Achieving such a balance is a challenge our team face every day while ghost-writing columns and commentary articles for our clients. Yet writing for others offers a shortcut. We can interview the expert being bylined, transcribing the recording and then removing our (hopefully intelligent and well-ordered) questions (perhaps turning them into crossheads). This gives us a first version in the expert's authentic voice, which can then be edited for meaning, grammar and emphasis. It usually needs shortening, and the sections require stitching (once ordered correctly). Yet if our word-surgery is executed skilfully we'll have succeeded in retaining our client's genuine voice while also removing the inevitable glitches.

It's how we train our "ghost-writers" (a term I dislike, feeling that it demeans their craft) — giving them an advantage over freelance journalists who have a well-honed writing style of their own that they apply to all their writing no matter who's awarded the byline. The results — as we've discovered on numerous occasions — feel divorced and neutral, like white paint. Meanwhile, our trainees produce content rich in texture and clearly from our clients.

Of course, the above also works for the authors themselves. If you're comfortable with your speaking voice — perhaps from presenting at many industry events — then preparing a series of questions and recording and transcribing the answers may be a strong way to start any writing project (and another potential route for over-coming writer's block).

Avoiding the "breezy style"

Retaining our voice is challenging from both ends of the language spectrum: turning vernacular verbiage into universally understandable text and converting mechanical *PowerPoint*-speak into something written by a human being rather than a machine.

A brilliant example of the former appears in the classic work from Ronald Blythe called *Akenfield*. Written in the late 1960s, Blythe's work (later made into a landmark film) consists of interviewing elderly villagers in rural Suffolk — recording the harsh endeavours of people born before 1900 who'd spent their lives working the land. Try this passage from 72-year old farmworker Leonard Thompson.

> "There were ten of us in the family and as my father was a farm labourer earning thirteen shillings a week you can just imagine how we lived. I will tell you the first thing which I can remember. It was when I was three — about 1899. We were all sitting round the fire waiting for my soldier brother to come home — he was the eldest boy in the family. He arrived about six in the evening and had managed to ride all the way from Ipswich station in a milkcart. This young man came in, and it was the first time I had seen him. He wore a red coat and looked very lively. Mother got up and kissed him but Father just sat and said, 'How are you?' Then we all had tea, all of us staring at my brother."

And this one from 79-year-old horseman's widow Emily Leggett.

> "I have been wed and widowed twice. My first husband was head horseman at Round Wood Farm and when we married his wages were thirteen shillings a week. He used to give me twelve shillings and keep a bob for his pocket. We were children together, then lov-

ers, then I married him. He lived in the next-door double-dweller. We were both nineteen when we wed. A beautiful boy he was. It seems a long time now since I saw him. He had six horses to look after and he used to get up at five o'clock every morning to bait them."

Grammatically within reason, both are easy reads — both even including a recognisable inverted-pyramid opening. Yet their gentle Suffolk tones shine through the text, a masterpiece of transcribing and editing.

The temptation to write purely as we speak and even to instil folksiness into the text is what Zinsser calls the "breezy style" — a natural tendency of writers addressing informal audiences (maybe in a village newsletter with the villagers even addressed as "folks"). Yet it's a temptation he implores us to resist.

"Write with respect for the English language at its best — and for readers at their best," writes Zinsser. "If you're smitten by the urge to try the breezy style, read what you've written aloud and see if you like the sound of your voice" (he suspects you won't).

Injecting vim

Of course, in professional circles we're likely to face the opposite problem. That the language is too stilted — boxed-in by professionalisms and jargon. We deal with corporate-speak below, but how do we inject vim into speech that has less vigour than the computerised voice on *Google* maps (to use another era-constrained analogy)?

It's a problem we regularly face in PR, not least because many of our clients have English as their second language. Their authentic voice is in another language altogether and sometimes hidden beneath layers of jargonised platitudes.

While this supports the notion of writing being the "best us" because we have the time and space to perfect phrases and inject some life into stagnant prose, we also have to cope with the cadence and rhythms of our author's mother tongue being very different to the English we write on their behalf.

For instance, we have many native German speakers as clients whose first language requires exactness in the use of verbs and nouns, with three genders and four cases. There is also a sequencing within sentences that can seem overly formal or wooden when translated straight into English, even before the dead hand of *PowerPoint*-speak is added.

Our job is to soothe their speech as it appears in its written-English form: adding warmth while removing (perhaps an unconscious) reader-acquired accent when reading the text. Of course, this can be an uphill task when the author's name (written in the standfirst) is given as Jürgen Müller, *Hauptflaschenwäscher* (Chief Bottle Washer) at the *Bundesverfassungsgericht* (Federal Constitutional Court) or something similar. And, as with Blythe's Suffolk elders, there are times the accent or tone shouldn't be lost — maybe when writing for Silicon Valley entrepreneurs where imbibing their sunny Californian optimism could suit the text.

Indeed, we write for lots of Americans too, noticing the differences in sentence stresses, especially verbally, which can be a challenge for the transcriber. This goes beyond the well-known "upspeak" (or "high rising terminal") in which particularly younger Americans tend to inflect upwards at the end of a sentence as if they're framing a question.

While this irritates some (often older) listeners — who receive it as if the speaker is lining their speech with a certain incredulity towards the listener ("what do you mean you haven't heard of [insert obscure reference]?") — it has yet to significantly undermine written American-English, even if it needs editing out of some of our interviews.

As for the age-old American/British English debate: in the world of non-fiction — and particularly business writing — the differences are becoming barely distinguishable other than the different spellings (many deliberately generated by American lexicographer Noah Webster). There's the dilemma of Americans using nouns as verbs — loan, chair, gift etc. — and verbs as nouns — the reveal, the ask etc. But most British-English users now do the same. And there's also some residual differences in the use of tenses (saw/seen, ate/eaten) and prepositions (on the weekend/at the weekend), which need not detain us too long.

A more serious problem is that we've potentially contradicted our methodology from the previous chapter, in which we first write bullets before ordering and linking them. Except that we haven't. The bullets method is for writers unsure of their subjects or struggling with how best to articulate complex arguments and in what order. Most authors will tackle subjects like this when writing a major work, as have I below (on tackling corporate-speak). Other elements will come fluently and confidently and can flow straight onto the page before being (lightly) edited.

When applying the bullets, style will be an afterthought, though a vital one. Meanwhile, when our passages go straight on the page — with ease — we might need to tidy up the grammar and language to prevent the text being overly colloquial, all while managing to retain our authentic voice. The result should be consistently fluent writing: engaging yet authentic and with the right level of authority, and with the reader's journey smoothed throughout.

2.   Corporate and marketing speak

If you're expecting a diatribe against modern corporate and marketing language and its suffocating impact on good English, then you might find what follows *sub-optimal*. Writers are supposed to detest the buzzwords, stock phrases and jargon of 21st-century institutional life. After all, in part, it's what Sir Ernest Gowers was railing against in *The Complete Plain Words* back in the 1950s. And it's got a whole lot worse since.

Just about every "how to write" author detests such language, almost as a matter of course. Except this one. Why not me? Partly because I live in the real world and have to navigate corporate life every day. I was a banker in the 1990s, presenting papers to the compliance department and credit risk committee that relied on accepted terminology to ensure all readers understood what was being referred to — something Sir Ernest would have appreciated though many professional writers miss (Gowers's main aim was to simplify language and prevent deliberate obfuscation).

Not all jargon is redundant and some corporate phraseology can aid definition and understanding rather than detract from it. We just need to discriminate between what's acceptable and what's not. And we need to discern why we use certain phrases, ensuring our motives are the right ones.

So what's in and what's out? Some suggestions below.

OUT: long words when short ones will do. Sometimes, this is to do with cadence. Radio interviewees, for instance, often say "absolutely" when they mean "yes", which is usually due to interviewers, despite their training, asking closed questions. More often, long words are an attempt to sound more technical or learned. *Functionality* is a classic example. Try use or even *function. Transitioning* (change), *interface* (join) *econometrics* (the numbers), *disincentivise* (deter): in all cases, the shorter word eases the reader's burden and usually carries more punch.

OUT: compound words used to make the writer sound more important than they are or more technical than they need be. My use of *sub-optimal* above is an obvious example. Plain old *disappointing* would have been fine. Some are even invented portmanteau nouns or verbs: *upskill, downsize, rightsize, visioning, ideation, imagineer, disambiguate.* Kill them all.

OUT: phrases taken out of context, again in an attempt to add gravitas. This includes *actionable*, which is a legal term meaning something is prosecutable (i.e. "you have a case"), *cross-pollination, deep* *dive, weapons grade, red flag, marinate, sacred cow, soft pedal, tailwinds.* There are always more appropriate descriptions available without lapsing into appropriated terminology.

OUT: idioms and clichés used to sound pompous or as euphemisms for something not requiring a euphemism. *Above-board* (legal), *alignment* (agree), *on point* (correct), *bandwidth* (capacity), *washes its face* (viable), *put to bed* (complete), *put out feelers* (enquire), *throw under the bus* (blame), *soup to nuts* (all), *going forward* (in future), *give the nod* (agree), *human capital* (people/staff), *low hanging fruit* (easy wins), *the optics* (how it looks), *geographies* (locations), *reach out* (make contact), *touch base* (make contact, again). Bin the lot!

OUT: obvious pleonasms such as *pulse check* (check), *price point* (price), *pain point* (pain), *wiggle room* (room), *wallet share* (share), *value proposition* (value), *hard-stop* (stop), *covered off* (covered). There are hundreds of them.

So what's in?

IN: phrases or words that have meaning. *Competitive advantage* (while we could avoid the pleonasm by just saying advantage it matters over whom we have an advantage). *Out of pocket* (paid for by an individual, not a company); *digitalisation* (generating online processes that were formerly paper-based); *realtime* (when describing a process, such as a payment, happening without delay).

In fact, *realtime* is probably only borderline acceptable as is *gatekeeping* and *game-changing*. Each profession will have its own — the point being that the phrase not only has meaning within the context applied but cannot easily be substituted with a plain-English alternative.

IN: borrowed words/phrases that, nonetheless, describe something well. *Bespoke* is no longer exclusively for tailors (nor is *tailored*), nor *due diligence* only for lawyers. *Organic* works for growth generated using internal resources. *Post mortem* is no longer just for pathologists, *granular* has uses beyond baking (although *granularity* is horrid) and *execution* no longer involves an axe or rope. *Critical mass, bottom line, disintermediate, pipelines*: all have meaning despite being unloved by language snobs.

IN: neologisms (new phrases or words) that work even if unattractive. *Stakeholder* has come to mean everyone impacted by an organisation: owners, customers, employees etc. *Onboarding* describes well a necessary commercial process (as does *outsourcing* and *offshoring* and even *insourcing* and *reshoring*, horrid though they all are). And whether we like it or not companies do *micromanage, bootstrap* and *facilitate* and even potentially *future-proof, unbundle* and have *workstreams*. Again, the difference with those rejected is their relevance, brevity and clarity.

You may vehemently disagree with my in/out examples above, as well as wonder in which column your own industry's buzzwords belong. Yet the point I make is a simple one: we should think about the phrases and words we use. We should care about their real meaning as well as how they sound when read by our target readers.

If we want to sound like an insider — among our peers within an exclusive clique — then fine, go for it. Though we should certainly seek to improve on the lazy, suffocating and exclusionary examples that too often pepper the pages of professional or academic content. And we should also think about that new audience we're keen to capture.

Improving on insider speak

Let's look at a sample — something that crossed my desk this morning and is typical of the finance industry. And let's look at how we can improve it while not looking like an outsider.

"While many 'bank-agnostic' fintechs now offer SCF platforms that connect various parties with investors, this is an area BankX has operated in for some time. The bank already possesses a large, wide-reaching asset distribution platform that connects key parties

> along the supply chain in order to leverage excess liquidity. The platform also benefits from BankX honing digitalisation trends such as machine learning, artificial intelligence (AI) and automated machine reading as it lessens its reliance on in-person capabilities in favour of operational efficiency, scalability and cost reduction."

So how do we unravel such a concoction of clichés, jargon, acronyms and insider-speak? First, let's reduce the passage to its core messages. There appear to be two:

1. With respect to SCF platforms, BankX is well ahead of non-bank competition,

2. And to stay ahead BankX is automating its platform.

Yet even this makes little sense to the layperson, so we need some further unravelling, helping us also rebuild the passage into something more accessible:

> "Offering supply-chain finance (SCF) via online customer-facing platforms is a competitive area in banking and one attracting innovation from financial technology firms ('fintechs'). Yet BankX stays ahead of its newer rivals by utilising its global customer network and by adding innovations to its platform, including encouraging automation via artificial intelligence (AI). This makes BankX's offering more efficient and therefore cheaper than its rivals and helps it attract the widest number of users."

Of course, we could go deeper, by explaining automation and AI or by removing corporate words such as *utilising* and *innovation* (though both have meaning here). And insiders may already cringe at the replacement of *cost reduction* with *cheaper* (though the latter hints that the savings have been passed on to the customer).

There's also some information still missing, such as the platform's role of connecting investors and customers, though this can be added. What we should celebrate is the removal of pure gobbledegook such as *bank-agnostic* (I've no idea what this means, and the quote marks suggest that the writer is also unsure) and *in-person*; mouthfuls such as *wide-reaching asset distribution platform*; as well as obvious corporate-speak such as *honing digitalisation trends* and words such as *scalability*.

It's still not perfect: professional documents will never outrank Shakespeare or Dickens for eloquence. But they can be understood, accessible and readable.

Two tangential points on corporate language. First, companies are always singular, as are all institutions. "The Royal Navy is recruiting" not "The Royal Navy are recruiting" (amazing how often I have to correct this, even from seasoned writers). And companies are not equipped with eyes, so cannot see. "Ryanair see profits take-off ..." breaks both rules. And that also goes for years: "Last year saw..." being one of the most common red-pen transgressions to cross my desk.

Dealing with acronyms

And here seems the right place to tackle that other disease of modern writing: the three-letter acronym (TLA). They're everywhere and they're hated by writing purists. I once entered an article into a professional writing competition and had it humiliatingly thrown out thanks to a single unexplained TLA.

This made me detest the judge for his pomposity but, on reflection, he had a point. An unrecognised TLA is a major reader snag, often resulting in our poor captive reader having to track-back through the pages to discover its meaning. And that's assuming we followed the convention of spelling it out first use with the acronym in brackets.

For short articles, the SOFU rule (spell-out-first-use) is usually enough. But for anything longer, a better solution is required.

Some choices:

1. We could follow the pompous writing judges' instructions and ban them altogether — always spelling out the words,

2. For books and white papers, we could add a reference page or glossary of commonly used abbreviations, usually at the front,

3. We could follow the SOFU rule for every chapter or section.

There's no perfect answer, although I think a selective version of point three the best, perhaps allowing for three buckets of acronym.

Bucket one: for acronyms so common the spelt-out version is practically unknown, including ATM, BBC, CNN, DVD, GPS, HMS, PIN, URL (also BP, CNBC, HSBC, NASA and a few others that follow the same rule without being TLAs — just LAs). In fact, many of these are companies or organisations that are better known by their TLA (a common one in my world is the German lender KfW, which even some employees might fail to realise stands for *Kreditanstalt für Wiederaufbau*). The rule: just use the TLA/LA. But beware, their traction might be highly geographical or sector-specific.

Bucket two: TLAs that are common parlance (not sector-specific) though with the spelt-out version also regularly used. GDP, RBS, RSA, FBI, UAE etc. (again, this might be a highly subjective list). The rule: SOFU.

Bucket three: everything else, including *all* industry-specific TLAs. The point the pompous judge was making was that even specialist articles are not solely for insiders, or shouldn't be. He was right, of course, so TLAs should be either dealt with via a separate reference page or — my preference — SOFU+. This means SOFU plus periodic repeats of the full name, done smoothly and with aplomb. How often? Perhaps if there's been a gap of a chapter or so between usages.

Oh, and there's a bucket four: where TLAs shouldn't be used at all because they're lazy ugly text-language word-substitutes. BTW, LOL, POV, AKA and, indeed, TLA and SOFU all fall into this bucket.

3. Making it eloquent and compelling

We should strive for eloquence. Good writing helps us stand out from the crowd, especially in professional or technical circles that have an obsession with substance, usually to the detriment of style. See it as the soft-focus lens through which others will view us, or as the sharp suit or couture wardrobe that accentuates our skills as an executive.

As stated, this book is not a style guide. Nor is it akin to *Fowler's Modern English Usage*. There's more on both — and other useful guides and reference books — in the Appendix. But it is a book on learning to write excellent non-fiction. Given this, it's not enough to offer advice on process, as well as what to remove and avoid. We must also focus on what to add, as well as how to craft content to make it compelling.

A quick recall of what's already established. First, brevity: using Zinsser's brackets and similar devices to reduce our words to the minimum required while not losing our voice. Second, structure: including the application of the inverted pyramid to help grab the reader's attention. Third, some tricks such as sentence inversion and the judicious use of link words.

Yet we've still to consider beautiful writing — the construction of sentences and passages with such elegance and meaning that readers pause to read them again, not because of reader snags but due to their clarity, rhythm, fluency and even their beauty.

That should be our aim. Not simply to retain (or even detain) our readers — getting them to the end — but to delight them. To make our writing a pleasure to read. But here's where we need help. Luckily assistance comes from some brilliant writers, including etymologist Mark Forsyth.

His 2013 book *The Elements of Eloquence* dissects some of the most memorable lines and phrases in the history of the English language — from the *King James Bible* and Shakespeare to advertising slogans and pop-songs — and asks: what makes the perfect English phrase?

It appears that — consciously or otherwise — they're following certain rules. Here are six worth considering.

i. Alliteration

We're not talking "Peter Piper picked a peck of pickled peppers" which is alliteration that will open us up to ridicule. Most non-fiction works require gravitas, which limits the potential application of this device. But it shouldn't be ignored. The Peter Piper example had rhythm not because it rhymes but because the P sound is beating time, to the point you can almost hear the swinging arm of a metronome.

If we inject that into some of our phraseology we'll smooth the ride for our readers — turning jarring and difficult sentences into gently undulating passages.

We can even try it on our BankX example.

> "Encouraging automation by employing artificial intelligence attracts new users, allowing BankX to accelerate ahead of its rivals."

We shouldn't invent words or corrupt meaning, but we can choose the word order on that basis. And we should go easy: employing above could have been applying (in fact a more descriptive verb), but the rhythm works better by giving the As a rest, as well as allowing an alliterative subplot to develop with the Es.

Headlines are a fruitful area for alliteration even if they need to avoid journalese, which can sneak into headlines almost unnoticed. Examples such as "Bank's bonus bonanza breaks all records" will certainly undermine our work (*bonanza* being a word Waterhouse would hate and is only there because it begins with B).

But "Record year for bank bonuses thanks to bonds, buyouts and equities" works with *thanks to* preferred over *because of* to give us a break from the Bs, as well as being a more descriptive conjunction.

And for the title of our white paper or book, alliteration is almost a must. Forsyth points to works such as *A Christmas Carol*, *Sense and Sensibility*, *Pride and Prejudice* and even *Where's Wally?* that are immediately memorable, as well as an intellectual landgrab over a particular subject. And they work for just about any sector.

> *The Future of Finance,*
> *The Trouble with Teaching,*
> *Making Museums Memorable,*
> *Taking Technology Forward.*

Add a generic and descriptive sub-heading and you immediately have something that jumps out as important, relevant and readable, which — given all the work you've put into it — is exactly what your writing warrants.

ii.   Tricolon

Known as the "rule of three", this is an oratory trick that pre-dates Cicero. It's also writing's equivalent of the golden ratio in art and mathematics (1.618). Indeed, the tricolon is the golden rule of memorable and compelling writing.

There are hundreds of examples: *The Good, the Bad and the Ugly*; *eat, drink and be merry*; *the Father, the Son and the Holy Ghost*; *Life, Liberty and the Pursuit of Happiness*; *life, the universe and everything*; *mad, bad and dangerous to know*; *Liberté, égalité, fraternité* — I could go on and on (and on). It's all about rhythm. So much so that one of the three can often seem like a stretch or repetition: *Friends, Romans,*

Countrymen; *Government of the People, by the People, for the People*; *I came, I saw, I conquered.*

As Forsyth points out, the *tricolon* is so strong that it's even shoe-horned into our memory of great lines. Churchill's "blood, toil, tears and sweat" is remembered as "blood, sweat and tears" while Thomas Hobbes's "nasty, brutish and short" also included "solitary" and "poor" when describing the life of ordinary souls in *Leviathan*.

So find your *tricolons*, whether in the titles or the text. They will make your prose both more readable and more memorable. And they're a must when listing attributes. If we return to our BankX example we can see that its AI offering makes the bank "more efficient than its rivals, cheaper, and more able to attract the widest number of users". Just three attributes then, not four or two? Funny that.

And notice that the order of the syllables creates a rhythm sandwich: *longer, short, longest-of-all*. Rhythm dictates that the longer element often comes last — *dangerous to know*; *pursuit of happiness*; *we band of brothers* — but not always: *wine, women and song*; *snap, crackle and pop*; or Dorothy Parker's requirements of a man, that he be "handsome, ruthless and stupid".

iii. Epizeuxis

Talk about going on and on (and on) brings up a further rule of three (or four, or five), this one more a figure of speech although it can work in extended form on the page. One of Tony Blair's most remembered speeches included the *epizeuxis* "education, education, education" and one of Margaret Thatcher's "no, no, no". Firebrand orator Ian Paisley famously shouted "never, never, never", which was bettered by Churchill who cried "never give in, never, never, never, never" showing that *epizeuxis* — pronounced with the middle *zeux* emphasised — is not restricted to a three-times repetition.

Can *epizeuxis* work when read within the body of serious writing? Well, its close associate *anaphora* certainly can. This is a repeated word or phrase at the beginning of consecutive sentences. Again, this also works best for speeches (think of Churchill's "we shall fight them on the beaches") though it can also generate a strong rhythm for a summary passage:

> "Check the amount, check the address, check the recipient — and then, and only then, check back with the customer."

In fact, it also works in reverse, ending each clause with the same word. This is called *epistrophe* and is a device of songwriters of all eras: "when the moon hits your eye like a big pizza pie, that's amore" etc. etc. Forsyth points to Shakespearian examples including Othello's "a fine woman! A fair woman! A sweet woman!" though Macbeth's "o horror, horror horror" is an *epizeuxis*, as is Joseph Conrad's "the horror, the horror" (also used in the 1979 movie *Apocalypse Now*).

For Brits, one obvious example of *epistrophe* is the national anthem.

> "God save our gracious Queen,
> Long live our noble Queen,
> God save the Queen!"

Though probably the most perfect political example in recent years was reported by Martin Sixsmith, then a Whitehall communications officer. He revealed the considered opinion of civil servant Richard Mottram regarding a potential PR problem at his department.

> "We're all fucked. I'm fucked. You're fucked. The whole department is fucked. It's the biggest cock-up ever. We're all completely fucked."

All of which is, I suspect, Sixsmith's brilliant editing of Mottram's real, though certainly expletive-laden, verbal appraisal of the situation.

Less profanely — and returning us to the cause of good writing — epistrophe is a natural aid for structuring the chapter or section ahead, especially if posed as a series of questions.

> "If the future of employment is all about sustainability then we have some questions to ask. Is where we work sustainable? Is what we do sustainable? Is whom we employ and how we promote them sustainable?"

All of which generates an immediately memorable structure that triggers anticipation in the reader, as will our next device.

iv. Segue

Segue is an Italian word meaning "follows" though it has come to mean a link or pivot between two subjects: most famously used by TV anchors trying to link the soap opera just finished to the quiz about to start.

> "Poor Deirdre. Perhaps her problems would be solved by becoming a millionaire. Up next — who wants to be one?"

If done well, it can also work for our writing — encouraging readers to make that leap between chapters or sections and also helping stitch our structure together. If done poorly (as in the example above) it can irritate, even fostering a low-level contempt in your abilities as a writer.

When using this device to jolly-along the reader, caution is therefore required.

Segues are most common in music (hence being an Italian rather than Greek word), allowing a smooth transition between two passages of music in a concert, opera or rock album (*Pink Floyd* famously used them throughout their later albums). And that's probably how best to think of them here: a smooth transition. They're the bridge between two subjects and, as such, should be streamlined, direct, appropriate and hopefully elegant.

> "If automation is the trend keeping the chief technology officer awake at night, diversity — covered in the next section — is what's bothering the head of human resources." (see also antithesis below).

> "It's no coincidence that the church and the manor house nestle within adjacent plots on the main road through the village. And, having explored the Norman church, let's slip through that discreet wrought-iron side gate to explore the medieval mansion next door."

> "Having completed our first draft, we should congratulate ourselves — before realising we now have to go back and edit our work from the beginning."

While all three work, the first could be an inappropriate comparison (does automation really induce insomnia in CTOs?) and the second too florid, though both effectively make the switch. But the third is the Goldilocks example: adding the congratulations to soften the stark pivot while subtly introducing the next subject, all of which goes to show that "practice makes perfect".

v.   Proverbs, idioms, similes etc.

Statesman Lord John Russell described proverbs as "the wit of one, and the wisdom of many," which is both a proverb and an antithesis (see below). But are they useful for the writer — perhaps looking to explain a difficult concept or maybe make a philosophical point to break up the wall of research or data being presented?

Well, it depends. Proverbs (traditional sayings — "ignorance is bliss" "practice makes perfect" etc.); idioms (figurative expressions — "add fuel to the fire" etc.); similes (comparative figures of speech — "bright as a button" etc.) can all help bolster meaning. But, if poorly applied, they can equally jar awkwardly or clash with the voice we've spent time honing.

Throw them in for embellishment or to dilute heavy passages that should simply be better written or as a means of showing off, and the reader will mark you down as an amateur. Use them as the sharp end of a searing passage, and the reader will be rewarded with a strong understanding of your point and a familiar trigger for their memory.

So what works and what doesn't? Certainly — and if you'll excuse the idiom — less is more when it comes to all three. Overusing figures of speech to improve your style treats style "as if it were something that you could buy at the store and drape onto your words in bright decorator colours," says Zinsser, slipping in a simile at the end for good measure (whoops — another idiom).

As you can see, writers have to work hard to prevent the floodgates opening (sorry) with respect to such phrases. And that must surely mean that some uses are acceptable — even helpful — and that we just need to know where to draw the line (enough, enough!).

While Zinsser disliked all three, he thought idioms the least dislikeable, especially if offering a flavour of the vernacular — that is, writing to reflect a particular oral heritage. In this case, they can add richness and humour, and certainly voice, though he was down on idioms strung together in lazy journalese — fingering sportswriters as particularly guilty, not helped by sports stars famously speaking in such fashion when being interviewed ("over the moon" "sick as a parrot" and the like).

In the highly-regarded *The Elements of Style* by William Strunk and E.B. White, the author's sniffily refer to similes as "a common device and a useful one" though we're warned that "similes coming in rapid-fire, one on top of another are more distracting than illuminating" — and more suitable for Shakespeare sonnets than strong non-fiction writing.

Let's apply some nonetheless, returning to BankX.

"Though threatened by the speed of the quick-off-the-mark [idiom] fintechs, BankX sought to play a long game [idiom], remembering that slow and steady wins the race [proverb]. Ultimately, combining its AI technology with its network stole the march [idiom], acting as the rocket fuel [simile] the bank needed to beat the fintechs hands down [idiom]."

As we can see, one idiom is fine — potentially helpful — while four are indigestible. And while the simile adds a welcome visual prompt, using rocket fuel to win hands down not only sounds dangerous, it commits the rookie error of being a mixed metaphor. Also, the proverb makes the passage clunky and archaic: acting more as a reader snag.

And finally, there are metonymies: figures of speech that act as interchangeable alternatives, allowing the writer to avoid repetition. Many of these are geographic. *Wall Street* or *The City* when meaning finance, *Whitehall* when meaning the civil service (in Britain) or the *Oval Office* when referring to the American president. Of course, some of these are now dated: London and New York's financial institutions are just as likely to be in Canary Wharf or Connecticut, and British civil servants are scattered nationwide. But the meanings remain — for now — and can add a refreshing alternative when focused on a single topic involving the same institutions.

Of course, a metonymy differs from a synecdoche, which is the use of a part of something to describe the whole: hands instead of people for instance. We often interchange bank names such as Barclays and Santander with the *Bank* or even *the lender* or — at a stretch — *the financier*. Why? Because repetition is considered a crime against good writing, resulting in what tabloid journalists call *knobbly monsters*. The term comes from a notorious article in *The Sun* in which a journalist needed to find an alternative to the word crocodile in an article about a fatal attack from said water-dwelling carnivores.

You can see the problem, though it's important that, when dealing with repetition, the solution isn't worse than the crime.

vi. Antithesis

Forsyth covered neither segues nor the use of proverbs (perhaps because both lacked an unpronounceable Greek-derived descriptor) but he did cover the antithesis, of which Oscar Wilde was the champion.

"Wicked women bother one, good women bore one."

"Journalism is unreadable, literature is not read."

"If one plays good music, people don't listen, and if one plays bad music, people don't talk."

You get the idea. We pose one point and then juxtapose it immediately with another, not necessarily offering the inevitable Wildean twist.

As with *epistrophe*, there's some structuring assistance within, at least if we complete the Hegelian notion of our thesis and antithesis requiring a middle-way synthesis as a resolution.

"Businesses must be ethical. But being ethical is usually unprofitable. How can we resolve this conundrum and make our businesses both ethical and profitable?"

This a rhythmic opening and a memorable one. And it's an obvious precursor to a ten-point plan.

Yet antithesis triggers a punctuation debate. Should we divide the two clauses using a comma, a colon or a full stop? I'm neutral on this, as I am on many other issues of punctuation, although I'm grateful for the segue into the next section.

4.   A brief word on punctuation

Inconsistency is the worst punctuation crime of all. Readers might find your use of semi-colons and dashes irritating but they'll come around if you're consistent. Like most aspects of English, the hard-and-fast rules are remarkably pliable and in some cases contradictory. But readers want to settle into a style and not be jolted from it through some random re-engineering of your formatting or the whimsical application of punctuation.

Within limits, each book may have sovereignty over its own rules though they should apply throughout the book and potentially across all your writing.

At least, that's my opinion. But beware: punctuation is the realm of the pedant (obsessives for correct details), the most famous of whom is Lynne Truss, author of the 2004 "book of the year" *Eats Shoots & Leaves*. She prescribes a zero-tolerance approach to punctuation although, in reality, the same elasticity that makes English such a remarkably pliable language pervades even her work.

For me, punctuation marks are the road signs for readers. Just as crossheads and standfirsts are the sign-posts to a destination, punctuation marks are the white lines and cat's eyes in the road as well as the triangular warning signs. They warn of sharp bends and bumpy passages and are there to keep the reader on track and heading forwards.

Yet controversy reigns. Some of the bigger issues below.

The exclamation mark

Just about every writing-style guru comes down hard on the exclamation mark (exclamation point to Americans). Once reserved for screaming tabloid headlines and distress scenes in fiction, thanks to social media and text messaging it's now a ubiquitous signal for anything other than a dead-pan sentence, much to the annoyance of grammarians everywhere.

Given the difficulty in judging tone in short-form messaging (such as text and email) — and the consequences for getting it wrong — its overuse is forgivable, though even here the exclamation mark is often deemed too subtle and is being replaced by face emojis that relay various states. But for long-form content, immediate tone-signalling should be less important, allowing us to revert to its use as an indicator of sudden drama. "Help!" "Never!" "Absolutely not!" rather than as a means to express irony or humour, which — if requiring the aid of an exclamation mark ("joke here!") — was probably not as amusing as we'd hoped.

The dash

The dash, or em-dash if being typographical — meaning the longest of the three available dashes (the others being the en-dash and the hyphen) — causes as much controversy as the exclamation mark, and divides opinion among grammarians. Its correct use, as in the sentence above, is to add a sub-clause within a sentence, requiring both an opening and closing em-dash. Yet note that both of the above sentences (and this one) possess sub-clauses, so what divides the em-dash from the comma (or from brackets)?

My view — and it's just a view — concerns the direction of travel for the reader. Are you making them stop to consider another point? Then use em-dashes. Are you adding a gentler aside or a reminder? Then put it between commas, especially if — when reading it back — it can work without the commas. And if it's a clause nudging its way in, in a "don't forget me" kind of way (or maybe reminding the reader of a prior point or something ahead) then use brackets.

Of course, the second use of the em-dash — and the more controversial one for grammarians — is when introducing a second half to a sentence. This is an additional clause rather than a sub-clause that, with some thought, could probably be turned into a new sentence. It's a change of direction, potentially even an antithesis, and it's telling the reader that something exciting is being bolted on — something that simply cannot wait. Shouldn't this be a colon? Maybe, but colons are for lists. They are asking the reader to take a breath before continuing. The em-dash is saying, "hold onto that breath — this is interesting".

One tip: if the second clause is introduced by the gerund of the verb (with the *ing* ending), it could suit an em-dash, although it could also be a comma, depending on the extent to which it reads like a new clause rather than just an add-on.

The colon

As we've established, colons are for lists, though not always. As the para above reveals, it can also introduce an extended point the writer feels needs to be heralded in such a way. Normally, the colon-break in a sentence means that a list is coming, usually broken by commas rather than semi-colons. That said, just as inverting sentences can make them more compelling, so can inverting lists. To gain readers' attention, to excite and to tantalise: listing first can occasionally work better than the other way around.

The semicolon

This is a Victorian device and should be put out of its misery, says Zinsser. In fact, he said "use it with discretion", though offered no practical uses that were not likely to be better served by a dash or a full stop/period. Truss puts herself in the "save the semicolon" camp before detailing the number of writers that want it expunged from their toolbag. She also points out that the semicolon is Medieval (or Early Modern depending on your crossover year) and therefore not a modern affectation, although she does an unconvincing job of defending it.

I personally dislike semicolons but I'm willing to defer to a mediator, which — given that we're writing non-fiction for a non-literary audience — should be *the* authority in such circumstances: *The Economist Style Guide*. "Use them to distinguish phrases listed after a colon if commas will not do the job clearly," it states while adding. "Don't overdo them."

I can't argue with that.

Italics

More formatting than punctuation admittedly but, again, something needing some rules if we're not to have random nouns and clauses italicised. The purpose of italicising text is to point out that it's somehow different — it's another mark in the road though one involving the road surface itself. It's saying "take note, this bit's different" usually because what's being italicised has provenance elsewhere.

Certainly, italicise the title of a book, film, newspaper or the name of a boat (though not normally a house or office, oddly). Other uses are to point out foreign words, particularly in French, Greek or Latin, and to emphasise certain words such as examples of what's under discussion in a sentence or occasionally to point out the best-in-class of a particular thing (such as *the* style guide, above). And that's about it (although I add software names such as *Word* for the purpose of clarity).

While we're on the subject, let's tackle the use of French and Latin phrases, which some writers love to use, usually to signal an expensive education (or to hide their lack of one). My view: don't. It rarely helps, often irritates and marks you out as a certain type of person. And if you must use them, please do this state-educated Essex lad a favour and add a translation in brackets. That way, everyone's happy.

Id gratum (appreciated).

Capitalisation

The Economist nails this one too. "The general rule is to dignify with capital letters organisations and institutions, but not people; and full names, but not informal ones."

So something like:

"Boris Johnson, United Kingdom prime minister, was previously foreign secretary but resigned from the Foreign & Commonwealth Office after disagreements with Theresa May's government during a Cabinet summit at Chequers, the PM's country retreat".

Should Cabinet be uppercase? Everyone seems to think so even though it somewhat breaks the rule (though there is a Cabinet Office). Yet, as *The Economist Style Guide* points out (quoting Ralph Waldo Emerson), "a foolish consistency is the hobgoblin of little minds," which is a bit of a pathetic get-out clause if ever there was one, although does somewhat sum up the debate when it comes to punctuation.

5. Considering SEO

These days — and unfortunately — no serious book on producing great content can ignore search-engine optimisation (SEO). I say unfortunately because the need for online articles to win a first- or second-page ranking on search engines such as *Google* (and a few others) results, almost universally, in alterations to our text that are based on attributes other than high-quality writing. Sometimes quite the opposite.

Can the damage be limited — meaning we can achieve the goal of receiving a high SEO ranking without compromising on quality? That's certainly the aim, and the basis for the (mostly positive) recommendations below: all of which come from working with clients on PR campaigns to propagate the articles we write on their behalf (known by the ugly phrase "content marketing" in the industry).

- Search engine algorithms, while constantly changing, are broadly focused on aligning their results as closely as possible to the query keyed into their search box. If the query asks "what are the best investment opportunities in Mexico?" and your article is headlined with that exact question, you stand a strong chance of ranking highly in the results,

- Yes, headlines count higher than body-copy with the algorithms, as do eyebrows, standfirsts, opening sentences and paragraphs, and even picture captions, all of which means that our focus on the inverted pyramid (repeating the key messaging or angle in the headline, standfirst and first sentence) is helpful — allowing the remainder of the body-copy to come through relatively unscathed by SEO requirements,

- Equally helpful is the fact the algorithms have learnt to dislike pure repetition (viewing it as "keyword packing"), meaning that — just as we've learnt to use different phrases and words to explain the angle (potentially three times in the first three elements) — so search engines will reward us for doing so,

- Positively beautiful is the fact search engines favour content that is focused on the "user experience" and targeting the searcher personally. Put simply, our early lesson on writing for an audience rather than simply unloading information, now pays dividends with respect to SEO,

- Less helpful is the fact synonyms and metonymies (*asset* for *investment*, *"south of the border"* for *Mexico* etc.) can downgrade an article, which is a challenge — though one that has to be balanced by the need to also avoid "keyword packing",

- Also unhelpful is the downgrading of any variations in key terms — meaning that *Mexican* will be penalised as will *Mexico's*. That said, the algorithms are constantly learning, so this may quickly become a dated concern. And it's less true with verbs: *invest, invests, investing* and *investment* will all score well,
- And finally, crossheads should be generic and could even revert to being questions — indeed the Q&A or FAQ (frequently asked questions) format has become an SEO favourite.

Search engines such as *Google* claim their algorithms currently consider over 900 attributes when ranking content, with many of them focused on weeding out poorly written material (perhaps with poor syntax, clunky phraseology and shoddy grammar). All of which means we should travel in hope when it comes to SEO and good writing.

Chapter Six

Preparing for publication

We're now the proud owner of a completed first draft or manuscript (to use publisher parlance), written in a style we can call our own. Again, congratulations!

Yet we're far from done. Getting from here to a published book or white paper involves a further series of steps, all of which require the author's input. Dangerously, others now also become involved: copy-editors and proofers, designers and illustrators, as well as publishers and marketers.

All could have positive and helpful ideas about your work. They're the experts after all. Equally, they could apply discomforting preconceptions that send your work in the wrong direction. And while they might have in mind markets and audiences you haven't considered, which is great, they could also undermine your work's appeal to your core readership.

You're in charge of this process, remember — or you need to become so if you feel sidelined. This is your baby. And you know your core audience, which means their advice doesn't always hold. Listen, evaluate, absorb. But stick to your guns if you feel they've not understood your key premise or want to compromise your work beyond your comfort zone.

And, yes, I speak from bitter experience. Most published authors do, although I'm keen to point out that publishers are on your side. They'll just add different perspectives, which — while mostly valid — can clash with your own ideals. But it's your name on the cover so your voice counts most. And you might need to summon the courage to make yourself heard.

Caveats aside, let's roll on towards that very satisfying moment when what you have in your hands is a printed book or white paper (or at least a finalised and designed pdf if you're opting not to print, which would be a shame).

1. Proofing and editing

You do the first proof. But someone else should do the second, either a copy-editor at the publisher (or company, if publishing a white paper) or — if self-publishing — someone you've paid to do the job. Don't skimp, although do make them track changes — they could've missed something subtle in the writing.

What should your proof be concerned with? We dealt with the facts and quotes earlier, though don't be too proud to check any nagging doubts again. Once published, factual errors are hard to correct and can even, in extremis, lead to added erratum (correction) slips within every printed copy or — more likely these days — having the entire print run pulped. Libel issues and plagiarism are the other pulping offences, so make yourself comfortable on both counts: it's your work, no one else will care as much or have the same insight with respect to the potential concerns.

What else? Well, a big job will likely be the wordcount. Most writers start a project wondering how they'll ever manage to meet the wordcount required. And they end up wondering how they'll ever manage to cut the wordcount back to the agreed length.

Yet that's all part of the process. Draft one was always meant to be the freer you — the expressive you. It was bound to get out of hand. But the party's over. Now the clean-up begins. And cutting it to length is job Number One.

Some tips:

- Remember Step Six in our Writing by numbers chapter. If you delete the first sentence of a section does it still make sense? What about the second — even the first para? Second para? Don't stop until you are at the bone, not least because it's surprising the number of times this almost immediately cuts you to length,

- Now the other end. Journalists employing the inverted pyramid are trained to write allowing sub-editors to cut from the bottom, and this might work for each of your sections. If you opened, as recommended, with the conclusion and built your case from the most critical points down then the later points might be dispensable,

- Also, conclusions can be added out of embarrassment. You've finished, what now? Let's summarise. No need. Delete it for a one-line segue into the next section,

- Nearly all first drafts include passages that the writer reads again several times wondering whether it's right to include them. We now have our answer: it's not — kill them. One of my first sub-editors told me as I complained about some savage subbing "you have to kill your babies in this game". He meant that any favourite phrase or *bon mot* — any passage you're particularly proud of — is almost certainly superfluous. As Stephen King wrote in *On Writing*: "Kill your darlings, kill your darlings, even when it breaks your egocentric

> little scribbler's heart, kill your darlings",

- And what about those cherished quotes from respected figures? They support your points and bolster your confidence. But they're usually repeating a point you've just made or are about to make. One or the other can go,
- Anecdotes tend to do the same. While both anecdotes and quotes can lighten the weighty substance of your text, clever writing can ensure they make the point rather than repeat it. If they can't, perhaps they're more tangential than you think.

And if all that fails, remember Zinsser's brackets, removing superfluous words and clauses. Certainly, most passages can be tightened on second reading, although we'll need to ensure that the tightening is applied evenly throughout. Flaccid paras full of rolling passages followed by taut prose will leave the reader confused — wondering which style is the real you. So make it the taut one throughout.

A final point. If all the above sounds painful, it is. But it's less painful than having a jobbing copy-editor at the publisher do the cuts. If your efforts resemble the skilled knife of a Harley Street specialist the publishers' will seem more like the hacksaw of a battlefield surgeon. If you don't want to lose whole limbs and even the odd vital organ do the job yourself, not least because your professionalism in delivering the correct word length will impress, which could come in handy for the battles ahead.

What the copy-editor saw

And with the wordcount met, we can move on to more detailed work. This involves two further edits, concerning:

1. Typescript consistency,

2. Typos.

We're now doing the copy-editor's job for them, although the cleaner the draft we hand over, the better the impression we'll make.

They'll likely be applying the publisher's house style on particular aspects of the text, ensuring consistency throughout. Indeed, for all the elements below, it's worth asking for a copy of your publisher's style guide (again, they'll take note of your professionalism).

And if you don't (yet) have a publisher or are self-publishing, follow *The Economist's* style guide. It rarely errs and is highly readable. Another book worth buying is *Butcher's Copy-editing*, which is often cited in proofing and editing circles, though beware: *Butcher's* is Gibbon's *Decline and Fall of the Roman Empire*, to *The Economist's Carry On Jeeves*. It's a fine reference book but a weighty tome. Bedtime reading (unless you're an insomniac), it ain't.

So here's a flavour of what they'll focus on and how we can perhaps pre-empt them.

Spelling

American or British? It goes a little deeper than that. For instance, debate rages over the use of the S or Z in organise/ize, realise/ize, privatise/ize and the like. British English users tie themselves in knots, with purists arguing that *ize* is correct according to the *Oxford English Dictionary*, only to have it corrected to *ise* by proofers, who declare *ize* is American spelling.

It's not: both British and American English follow the same rule. The suffix *ize* is for verbs denoting a transformation, so a simpler version of the word exists: *theorize* (theory), *legalize* (legal), *nationalize* (national) etc. This is the majority of uses. Meanwhile, the suffix *ise* is for words that are not transformative verbs: *advise, comprise, despise, disguise, revise, surprise* etc.

Is that settled then? Well, no: *ise* spellings on words such as *organise* are now so embedded in British English that manuscripts with the *ize* spelling will often be corrected. Kingsley Amis in *The King's English* — a stickler in most things — opines that the *ise* suffix can nowadays be used "without a second thought". And while most respected book publishers follow the rule above, both *Butcher's* and *The Economist* opt for the ise spelling, after some agonising. And most spell-checkers accept both.

I was even told the British-English transformation began with Fleet Street hot-metal typesetters regularly substituting the letter S, having run out of Zs, though that could have been a cub journalist's equivalent of being sent out for stripy paint and air hooks.

Otherwise, use British English unless it's an American publisher or client. Yet — as with all things trans-Atlantic these days — the divisions are rapidly narrowing. We work for several American banks and have to sweep through the copy at the end checking for and removing U from colour and inverting the re for centre etc. Yet, in the grand scheme of things, the differences are minor and easily found.

Last thing on this: proper nouns stay in their original spelling. The Department for Labor in the US is spelt without a U on both sides of The Pond (to use a metonymy). Same with the Department of Labour in the UK (now gone, though still operating in South Africa): the U stays. Both the Rockefeller Center in New York and Centre Point in London will always have their original spellings, no matter where they're being published.

Quotation marks

Annoyingly, the British book publishing style is single quotes for any quotations and double quotes for quotes within quotes, 'he told me the chicken was "a little rubbery" but I disagreed' — sort of thing. Yet that's for book publishing. I'm from a magazine and newspaper background, which mostly does the opposite. And that feels right to me.

Thus, I sulkily hand in my manuscript to book publishers with double quotes and they dutifully convert them to single quotes, which somewhat undermines my professionalism, though I suspect I'm not the only person trained to write for periodicals that considers the book world's system all wrong.

Then there are quotation marks for phrases or idioms with a nameless source rather than actual quotes. Use these sparingly. If a regular phrase or cliché, quotes can probably be avoided (as should most clichés, come to that). Quote marks have a key use in these cases: for sign-posting phrases that, while common parlance for insiders, might need pointing out to the rest of us. They can also be used to distance the writer from the statement — as if putting on rubber gloves to insulate yourself from something disagreeable.

Mostly, quote marks are classic "bumps in the road" signposting for readers. For instance, in Chapter One, para one, I write: "What's meant by the 'book in them' aphorism is that everyone has something to say". With the quotes removed, the sentence would become awkward — a reader snag — hence the quotes guiding readers around the phrase, although hyphens (book-in-them) could have also done the job (see hyphenation below).

Singles or doubles for the idioms? Make them the same as the full quotes (so singles if following UK book publishing norms, doubles if — like me — you're not).

Hyphenation

Only slightly less controversial than spelling and quotation marks. Again, we should see hyphens as reader guides to smooth otherwise bumpy passages. I was taught that hyphens are for when we're adding to a noun or verb to make a new noun or verb. The example given to me was *chalk-up board*, while *Butcher's* uses little-frequented place. If we'd left it *chalk up board* or *little frequented place* the reader might become confused (we could mean *chalk up-board* or *little, frequented place*). Here we're in no doubt: *chalk-up* and *little-frequented* are being added to a noun to create what *Fowler's Modern English Usage* calls "a single unit of meaning".

Butcher's also concerns itself with floating hyphens, using the example of *sixteenth- and seventeenth-century architecture*. Of course, without the word *architecture*, no hyphen is required.

Finally, the hyphenated phrase to help smooth aphorisms and idioms, as in the "book-in-them" instance above. It worked then because it did exactly as *Fowler's* prescribed: it created a "single unit of meaning" because "book-in-them aphorism" became the noun.

Question marks

Not controversial at all. Everyone is agreed: question marks are for direct questions (who is the president of France?), and that includes within quotation marks that might require a "she said" (lower case she) after the closing quote. Indirect questions — "my daughter asked me last night what I did in the war" — do not require a question mark.

Yet, as Lynne Truss warns in *Eats Shoots & Leaves*, question marks are increasingly encroaching into indirect questions, which a copy-editor will no doubt remove. Truss blames the now-notorious "upspeak" for this because it infers a "you know?" at the end of every statement, which is a trap worth avoiding.

Double spaces

Another easy one. Nearly all published manuscripts have a single space after the full-stop/period, not a double, despite what's taught in schools. So kill all the double spaces. In *Word*, a simple find-and-change will do the trick, something I have to do with trainees' copy until I can get them out of the habit.

Headings and crossheads

Here the copy-editor's sweep is for consistency and house-style. That all headings are in the same typeface, type size and style (italics/bold/ underlined etc). Changing it to a *sans-serif* typeface (if the body copy is *serif*) is another common page-design style, but — again — it needs to be done throughout. My preference is that the crosshead is different in just one aspect from the body copy: so is either a point or so larger, italicised or bold, but never all three.

That's if we're given the choice. Certainly, huge, bold, headline-style crossheads make the text look cheap and amateurish — but that's just my view. Publishers of non-fiction increasingly disagree.

Apostrophes

We now enter the deepest lair of the punctuation pedant. There are books aplenty dealing with apostrophes, with Lynn Truss's probably the most famous. I'll just settle one point, which has confused me over the years: Truss's or Truss'? Truss's view (quoting *Fowler's*) is that proper names ending in S require an S after the apostrophe — think *St. James's Park*. Yet this rule can be broken depending on the sound. She cites arguments over tennis player Jimmy Connors, with journalists routinely preferring "Connors' forehand" to "Connors's forehand", which sounds too much like a verbal tick when read aloud.

Yet errors are so common they (almost) stop being errors. Truss points to London's *St. Thomas' Hospital*, which spells its name in two-metre letters atop its main building, shouting its mistake across the river at the Houses of Parliament. *St. James' Park* — home of Newcastle United FC — does something similar, all of which suggests just how intractable some of these issues can be.

Typos

We could of course stay longer down the punctuation rabbit-hole but we need to move on — and there are plenty of books and guides, many of which (including my personal favourites) are reviewed in the Appendix.

Let's now look at typos. Every tiny error in the text that makes it into print should feel like a knife to your heart. You should hate them. Despise them. Allow them to ruin your life. Zero tolerance is not enough. Only a demonic absolutist approach is enough and you should make that clear to any copy-editor likely to handle your work between now and publication. But do not expect the copy-editor to find them all. In fact, they can be guilty of putting them on. Check their edits thoroughly. Most send through drafts with the changes tracked but even that can hide errors (such as double-spacing). And they can certainly misunderstand some of your more subtle points, even change meanings.

Writer Giles Coren wrote a now-famous letter to *The Times* sub-editors, railing against them removing the indefinite article "a" in a 2008 column for the newspaper, so that "wondering where to go for a nosh" became "wondering where to go for nosh". In doing so they destroyed a subtle *double entendre* regarding the street scene he'd spent the previous paragraphs constructing, which sent him into wild paroxysms of anger.

At the time I thought his response somewhat self-regarding, until my 2015 book *The Outside Edge* made a similar mistake through the change in the word "hero" to "here": a single letter error that turned an insightful comparison between the (somewhat exaggerated) outsider claims of George Orwell and Ernest Hemingway into an inarticulate sentence lacking rhythm.

Check again after any stage in which others have handled your text. For instance, page editors might want to remove a widow or orphan and will do so by editing the text, potentially brutally.

Proof and proof again: the removal of a single typo will have made the effort worthwhile.

Pronouns

We're far from done. The copy-editor's job involves a huge number of processes, all dealing with house-style issues such as abbreviations, cross-references, dates and times, measurements, money, numbers and many more: all to ensure your manuscript is fit to print. These need not detain us (though *Butcher's* is the book for you if you want to be detained).

Yet there's one contemporary issue worth mentioning: the thorny problem of pronouns. *Butcher's* captures this under its *Bias and Parochialisms* heading and calls it a "sensitive area where strong opinions may be held". So sensitive, that not having an opinion is considered an opinion, so you'll be glad to know I'm with *Butcher's* on this one. References to unnamed people should avoid the he/him pronoun even if it means rewriting the sentence. It's simply archaic to use sentences such as Ivor Brown's "the craftsman is proud and careful of his tools" when the *they* or *their* pronoun works just as well.

There's also the issue of titles such as *chairman* and *doorman* (and *craftsman*) that have all found preferable neutral replacements (such as artisan) no matter how awkward you think they sound. And even when referring to *man* as a concept — as in *early man* — it's now possible, as well as universally preferable, to employ alternatives such as *early humans*. Even *manpower* is easily replaced by *staff* or *workforce*.

These are old words and phrases. And, while not necessarily offensive — they were the common parlance of their day — that day has passed and they increasingly make authors using them appear dated.

2.   Graphs and tables

For professional writing projects, supporting graphs are often essential — sometimes even central to the text. That said, I dislike reading documents that are led by graphs with the text simply linking Table 1.11 and Graph 2.12. The text ends up feeling like filler, with the graphs telling the real story, in which case we should let them. By this I mean fill the pages with graphs with paragraph-long explanatory captions and maybe reduce the body copy to no more than a single linking sentence between them, potentially even starting and ending the sentence with the three-dot … punctuation.

A legitimate route, but it's not a book or white paper: more a presentation. For a writing project, far better to have a few clear graphs or tables that encapsulate your point and weave that into the narrative with the relevant point ending "(see table 1.1)".

But what style of graph? The cleaner and simpler the better, in my view. This isn't saying don't be imaginative — you don't have to restrict yourself to bars, columns, pies and lines. But don't corrupt the core purpose of the chart, which is to visually relay comparative information.

Certainly, we shouldn't over-complicate the information being presented when our goal is the opposite. I recently edited a newsletter in which one of the analysts proudly displayed an admittedly important statistic (a percentage) as if it were a petrol gauge: the arm pointing at 28% on a semi-circular dial. His problem, he said, was that the statistic mattered and he wanted to display it well.

I pointed out that, far from displaying it well, he'd made it look ridiculous. Not one of his readers needed the concept of 28% explaining: they get percentages! His approach was the equivalent of ruining cat photos by making them wear a tutu, I told him, and instead recommended he just used a pull-quote to highlight the figure (see below).

By imaginative, I mean thinking about the type of chart that best illustrates the data you want to present. As well as bars, columns and lines, there are spiral charts and funnel charts and polar charts and bubble charts and scatter charts and percentage stacked bar charts — all available on most software packages (that page designers can convert into something smart). And, of course, there are simply tables, which often work best.

Each table or chart needs a number and a readily understandable title: as generic to the graph's purpose as possible. But it needs little else. As stated, let the text do the talking. The graphs are either complementary to the body copy or they're superfluous.

Again, *The Economist* is the authority on this. It usually presents just one chart per story with that chart brilliantly encapsulating the issue under discussion. And it's usually in a style that best conveys the point being made, with the body copy — all the while — the master and the graph the servant.

3.   Images, illustrations and maps

In our over-stimulated world, images are the attention grabbers. Plain text is just too dull to do the job. Consequently, very little is published nowadays without supporting images. Good images can enhance good writing, making content stand out as compelling. Yet the opposite is also true, meaning that this is not something to ignore or leave to the publisher — images matter.

And they're worth investing in. Amateur shots are fine if your photography is up to it. If not — and budgets are tight — try sourcing from a free library such as the non-profit Creative Commons (*creativecommons.org*). Creative Commons allows artists and photographers to share their work, and for publishers to use them, with accreditation but without cost.

There's an extensive library (1.6 billion items and counting), often connected to *flickr*, though beware: some (in fact most) stipulate non-commercial uses only. That said, there's an open dialogue with the artist/photographer who may well be persuaded of your cause or ask for a small donation.

Yet real quality can be hard to find, meaning you might have to go professional. Shutterstock offers five-image packs for £29 (2021 prices) that can professionalise any white paper. Our banking white papers often use City of London or Wall Street shots as standard. Could we be more creative? Sure, but these are generic photos for a financial white paper: themes are often regulatory or compliance-related and being overly creative can quickly cross the line into being inappropriate or cheesy (people in suits shaking hands in atriums, kind of thing).

With images come captions. These are important. As stated, studies have shown captions to be the most-likely first text read by readers, which makes sense: the image being the most-likely page element to have grabbed the reader's attention. So make the caption something illustrative of the article — even potentially the fourth use of our inverted pyramid (after the heading, the standfirst and the first line). And no, it doesn't have to relate to the image, although it helps if it does.

A white paper on building standards for residential housing, for instance, could use an image of a typical "somewhere in Britain" housing development. This generates no obligation for a reference to anything other than the content of your white paper, though you could nod to the image as an opener.

"Desirable residences: sustainability as much as safety will drive future building regulations"

Other than photos there are illustrations, including sketches and line drawing. Both Creative Commons and Shutterstock have thousands, though be prepared to spend time pearl fishing. That said, it might be time well spent: a charming sketch can enliven text, though don't allow your imagination to run wild. One editing job I had on a financial magazine was for a science-fiction loving editor who chose fantasy images to add colour to the articles. We soon had inter-galactic planet scenes full of aliens and space rangers and bubble-pod cities illustrating articles on the World Bank or bond issues. And soon after that, the managing editor asked us to stop.

And make it appropriate. I still cringe at deciding to once illustrate an article on investment opportunities in Colombia with a photograph of footballer Andrés Escobar. It allowed me to make a pun in the caption about the risk associated with investing in the country but it was in poor taste. As one irate reader rang to point out, Escobar had been murdered in retaliation for scoring an own goal during the 1994 World Cup. I took the job a little more seriously after that.

Moving on, there seems to be something of an addiction for cartoons or satirical illustrations in papers and especially in presentations. For instance, if I was so minded I could pepper these pages with Dilbert cartoons as could most professionals (copyright issues allowing). Sure, they can amuse and even beat the picture captions at being the first element read. But that's the point. They're distracting. And they dilute the message.

What's more, they're usually only tangentially on-message. They certainly over-simplify, potentially belittling complex subjects. And they can even undermine your credibility. Why? Because they're nothing to do with you or your work and you're probably adding them out of insecurity.

Finally, maps. I love a good map. But I don't need to know where London is in the world or France is in Europe, simply because they're mentioned in the text. It needs to be both relevant to the text and information the reader needs and would appreciate. Home-drawn maps — perhaps of a village — need to be high-quality if they're not to harm the writer's credibility. Meanwhile, maps as graphs — perhaps coloured to denote differentiation in attributes — are great, though they can distort the point being made given population/land mass variations.

4. Cover image

The big question: what do we put on the cover? It'll define what's within more than anything other than the title of the work.

Some options:

- Nothing. Yes, nothing. Just white (or sometimes black) space. Make the typography work by using a strong typeface, well placed on the page. The result is often a very effective front cover. *Quiet* by Susan Cain (2012) is a fantastic example: embossed white text on a white background,

- A photo "to bleed" (taking up the whole page). Probably the most commonly chosen option, so be prepared to trawl through the photo libraries for what works. And don't accept an approximate fit — this relies on an "a-ha" moment or you might forever wonder if a better image could have been more effective. Sure, the publisher will have some strong ideas, especially if a white paper that's part of a series. But, as with everything the publisher says, care is required. Their ideas can also be awful and revealing. I always felt the front-cover image of my first published book (of a man in union-jack boxer shorts clutching dollars and a beer can) set me up for the criticism that followed, exaggerating the intended laddishness within (something my agent warned me of at the time),

- A single floating image. The cover of Joanna Penn's *How to Write Non-Fiction* contains just an old typewriter. It's perfect, which made me mad with envy (until I realised I could do something similar). *Get Things Done*, my book on personal productivity, has just a single tick. Again, perfect. These are also quite easy to source and do the minimum to distract the reader while remaining highly relevant. But please do make them relevant. Flowers, animals, sea-shells etc. rarely are,

- Artwork. If relevant, evocative and well-executed, why not? Penguin Modern Classics do this brilliantly, picking a painting that evokes the era and the mood. If fitting, it can even be more abstract, though fantasy sci-fi scenes or your niece's latest output probably won't cut it. Relevance is key and should be apparent. For instance, Roger Eatwell and Matthew Goodwin's controversial though hugely influential 2018 work on the rise of populism (called *National Populism: The Revolt Against Liberal Democracy*) had a line-drawing of a breaking wave, which left me unimpressed. Yes, I get it — but most won't and the cover's no place for a cryptic allegory. Is this the one place for a Dilbert cartoon? Not if I have anything to do with it but I can see the attraction.

My view: this is too important to leave to the publisher so take some time to think about what works — even visiting a bookshop or library and checking out relevant or rival titles. What hits the nail on the head? Then sell them the idea, even sourcing it yourself if required. At the very least, it will put pressure on them to come up with something equally strong.

5. Pull quotes

Usually in much larger type and boxed to disrupt the flow of the page, pull quotes are strong devices for attracting the reader and will compete with the picture caption for being the first-read elements on a page. They also need to be chosen by you rather than a page editor, who'll not have the same eye for the right quote.

If your text quotes others it's tempting to prefer them over your own words, although this is usually best resisted. Use *your* best line, not necessarily as (yet another) use for the inverted pyramid — more to tantalise or hint at the reward for reading the entire text. What's the jeopardy or implied threat within your angle? Perhaps a quote encapsulating that will have the biggest impact. 20-words max — usually shorter.

6. Boxed text

Many writers find boxed-out text annoying, as they should do. It destroys the long-form structure of content, preventing the building of the narrative para by para. So why are they so prevalent in non-fiction publishing? Because most non-fiction publishers perceive that readers prefer it that way.

Boxes full of related information — perhaps presented against a coloured background — are supposed to "break up the text", which always makes me ask "why on Earth do you want to 'break up the text'?" It assumes disorder-level attention deficits from readers without any evidence that such page-litter increases reader buy-in.

Fiction writers are never asked to do this so why the assumption that non-fiction readers have a shorter attention span? Readers are perfectly capable of reading content that starts at the beginning and ends, however many paras later, at the end — not least because crossheads can equally (in fact more sympathetically) do the job of guiding readers onwards.

Of my published books, the *What's Stopping You?* second edition includes the most boxed content, again at the publisher's insistence. I provided boxed summaries of each chapter, which I managed to keep to a single sentence: the "takeaway" in presentation speak. And I included some case studies, mostly of people who'd approached me after the publication of the first edition. For both, the boxes were relegated to the end of the chapter and did not interfere with the run of the body copy.

Certainly, if content can fit into the body copy, that's where it belongs. Boxes are for additional items that would interfere with the narrative of the core text: key-people biographies perhaps, or a list.

But boxed content is here to stay and, the chances are, your publisher or copy editor will expect you to provide both ideas and copy. So be prepared.

7. Appendices

Don't add guff for the sake of it. This isn't the place for the contents of a filing cabinet or the odds and sods that found no other home. Make them useful. I've decided on a quick and personal review of the books that have helped me as a writer and editor. Handy, I hope, but nothing too laboured.

The appendices run to 14 in *Butcher's*, some vital — such as publishers' proof correcting symbols (that many of my team wish I'd stick to rather than making up my own!). Others, such as the French Revolutionary calendar and Japanese historical eras after the Meiji Restoration, are no more than a curiosity, and are best left to old-fashioned almanacks. Pre-internet, this was justified. Now, start typing your query into *Google* and it'll almost certainly predict your question and provide the answer in seconds (though check that the source is reliable).

And that should guide us when it comes to appendices. Is there something not readily available — at least in organised form and from a trusted source — on the internet that could bolster your readers' understanding or provide further help? If so, great. Otherwise, give yourself a break — there's plenty more to be getting on with.

8.   Forewords, prefaces, glossaries etc.

As a reader my heart sinks when I pick up a volume to find a foreword from some eminent nobody, followed by a preface, followed by a preface to the second edition, followed by acknowledgements, followed by a lengthy and rambling introduction. In frustration, I find myself skipping to Chapter One and then spend half the book wondering what vital information I've missed.

What can we do to reduce all the guff that goes on before the book actually starts? One clue's in the page numbering. Most publishers don't start using Arabic (1,2,3) pagination until the introduction, meaning that everything else is an add-on and certainly not an integral part of the text. Let's deal with each of these offenders in their most likely sequence:

Foreword

This is usually from someone recruited for the job: the company chairman if a white paper or an eminent "name" if for a book — someone likely to grab our attention. They are there to add weight, which means the author is considered too lightweight to go it alone. My first self-help book even gave equal billing to my foreword writer, basically because they were famous and I wasn't (yes, publishers are that mercenary).

At least he wrote his foreword. In most cases the foreword is bylined to someone who's had no hand in writing it. At best, they're handed a draft to tinker with. At worst, they leave it entirely to a trusted junior, the publisher or even a PR agency. And, yes, I've written scores on behalf of people who'll never read them, leaving me convinced that we shouldn't inflict them on our time-constrained reader.

Preface

Just a foreword written by the author. So why haven't they written what they need to say in the chapters ahead? Two reasons (usually). It's a second or third edition and they're explaining the changes or some background to the changes. Or they've something to say about how the book should be read: some reader signposting, if you like, perhaps about tone or the angle or the mindset of the author that needs explaining. This can also include the author's justification for writing it: how they came to this point or something else they need to offload.

More often it's simply some self-indulgent anecdote about discussing a new edition over lunch at *Rules* or *Soho House* and how they insisted on writing it at their *gîtes en Provence*. Rarely, does the preface warm the reader to the writer, so — again — best avoided (note: the inclusion of one here falls into the reader-signposting and author-justification category and avoids the need for an introduction — not least because prefaces tend to be briefer).

Executive summary

Another element often forced upon writers, executive summaries make me want to shout "read it or don't read it — I don't mind which — but please don't half read it". That said, time-poor professionals might thank you, although the title of this book isn't *How to write for time-poor professionals*, which means I have no compunction in dismissing executive summaries as more pre-content fodder for people unlikely to ever appreciate good writing.

If forced to write one — and plenty of writers are — why not avoid the narrative form by making it a series of well-written bullets that tantalise rather than summarise? By making clear references to the structure of the book or (more likely) white paper, we are drawing in readers rather than listing spoilers.

- Part Two explores the myths built up around media-predictions of the 2008 financial crisis, with some of the most eminent commentators and economists claiming an after-the-event prescience despite well-documented bullishness right up until the crash.

By not naming those featured, we've hopefully piqued rather than satisfied curiosities.

Glossaries (including lists of abbreviations)

Tricky one. If you want to expand your readership — perhaps to become the guru on a complex or technical topic — a glossary of insider terms can be a comforting sight for a lay-reader (though make sure you get them right). Like a good map, it can help understanding and provide the framework upon which you build your case.

Yet they remain another roadblock to the core content, making my preference a quick explanation of insider references in brackets after first use within the text. Don't kill the flow: just add a tight definition (ten words max).

Of course, some readers may scream "I knew that — don't insult my intelligence" but most will either be grateful or simply skip over it. And it's better to keep a reader than avoid explanations due to fear of irritating a peer: after all, unknown words and phrases are the ultimate reader-snag — killing the reader journey stone-dead in many cases.

But my subject matter (helping non-writers write) isn't rocket science, so few items cannot quickly be explained within brackets or — if necessary — a footnote. More technical subjects may lend themselves more to a glossary than to having the body copy disfigured by too many bracketed explanations.

Acknowledgements

If books contained no acknowledgements, no one would be offended. The fact they do means you might feel obliged to thank the copy-editor and illustrator, the publishers, your agent, your agent's agent and Uncle Tom Cobley and all. For my first book, I even thanked the Puerto Rican sandwich maker in the deli and the east European waitress in the 86th Street diner. But I was being sarcastic.

And my instincts were right: unless there's a critical reason why someone needs to be acknowledged — perhaps someone who supplied much of the research and is not, for whatever reason, credited elsewhere — then there's no need. Everyone else is simply doing their job.

Dedication

Another minefield, so best keep it to the spouse and/or all the kids. I never really understood why I needed to dedicate my book to anyone, but — feeling I needed to do what I was told — dedicated my first book to my mum, who hated it and told me I'd live to regret it (she was right, of course).

Other junk

Some clever quote, bible scripture or *bon mot*, a line drawing of nothing in particular, a photo of your dog, child, car or second home, a Dilbert cartoon, a single frightening statistic meant to scare your readers from the off, two-sentence reviews from people you've cajoled into providing them. All, apart from the reviews (of which the best usually end up on the cover) should be avoided. It all becomes a bit self-regarding after a while, like a performer shouting "I love you all" to their audience while refusing to leave the stage (or, in this case, start the performance).

As for the quotes, publishers will always be keen for you to prostitute your contacts for supportive two-liners. And a surprising number will be happy to oblige, although some will ask you to write the quote. When asked, I'd focus on them and make sure they also got a plug: that way everyone got something out of it. Indeed, people peddling a book or research of their own are the best people to ask.

Table of contents and indices

At last! something worthwhile. A very good table of contents is vital in my view. This is your map, your executive summary and even your preface and indices all rolled into one. Not every crosshead needs to be listed, but every section and sub-section most definitely should, with the full headline written out. You owe it to your reader: pointing out the journey, the destination and the landmarks along the way. And it will also help with online versions that can be hyperlinked straight to the relevant content.

It can even save you needing an index, though I used to find a perverse OCD-type pleasure in collating my index, not least because publishers have a whizzy program for finding the page references (though it's prone to error, I've noticed). There's also a function in *Word* that collates tagged words and phrases at the end of the document, though doesn't translate the page numbers into the laid-out book template, which requires the publisher's software.

Self-publishers will either have to pay an indexer or do it manually, though it might be worth it. As the *Writers' & Artists' Guide to Self-Publishing* points out, "a good index is essential to the use of a non-fiction book; a bad index [or no index] will let down an otherwise excellent book".

As for the style of entry, this is — believe it or not — covered by an International Standard (ISO 999:1996 *Preparing Indexes to Books,*

Periodicals and Other Documents) and shows subjects starting with the differentiating proper noun with an indent for subentries.

Manchester, University of [in fact the *of* is optional], 2, **30-34**, 38, 47, 48, 51, 114
>Awards, 32, 48
>Campus, 30, 47
>Famous alumni, 34, 38, 51
>Origins, 2, 30
>Student life, 114

9.   The introduction

Do we even need an introduction? Why not just Chapter One? There might be some big-picture background or scene-setting that helps readers navigate the work ahead: "a long time ago in a galaxy far far away ..." sort of thing. Certainly, if your work is in four parts dealing with, say, North, South, East and West, there's certainly a role for something on The World (as defined by your subject matter), as well as where you're standing with that compass in your hand.

In this respect, introductions can work like an extrapolated version of the inverted pyramid, stating the angle and the conclusion with the chapters there to justify our assumptions. Most academic papers work this way. That said, introductions shouldn't be a written-out executive summary — something has to be held back for the committed reader.

You might lose some readers, perhaps those disagreeing with your angle or who find the premise irrelevant. But more will become committed because the introduction will have built their anticipation. Remember — our world isn't fiction, we don't need to build the suspense or add cliff-hangers. We need to justify and support our angle and prove to the reader that our content is relevant and worthy of their investment.

Sensible authors write the introduction last. By now you'll have both a beautifully fluent writing style and a clear picture of the project's entirety — allowing for that all-important helicopter view that the best introductions offer.

Yet introductions are also defined by what they shouldn't do. This includes:

- divulging too much detail about the chapters/sections ahead. Here's not the place for getting into the weeds, though we can refer to the chapters/sections that do,
- becoming a long-form version of an executive summary. The introduction is not a synopsis,
- introducing new content — perhaps a forgotten concept that occurred to you late on but doesn't fit into the structure. Save it for the follow-up book,
- being too personal. One anecdote about how you came to write this work is fine. Two or three starts looking indulgent,
- settling scores with rivals or doubters. I've seen it done and been tempted myself. But it makes you look bitter and insecure, so best avoided,
- engaging in debates with editors or co-writers that had a different view of the work. Again, I've seen it done — especially when works are co-written,
- becoming too sentimental, unless your work is one long sentimental diatribe, of course, though even then it might be refreshing to offer a rational framework before the mush takes over.

Yet none of the above should prevent you from concluding that the services of an introduction are not required. If you do include one, then be clear about its purpose as well as the fact it's adding value. Otherwise, it'll be yet more inconsequential verbiage before the reader can become acquainted with your key messages.

10. A conclusion

Same with conclusions. We dealt with chapter/section conclusions in Chapter Four, but the same equally applies here. Once you've said what you want to say, you can stop, perhaps with a line that makes it clear there's no more to come.

> And that completes our regulatory overview of banking digitalisation.

Done! Why add more? And why put it in its own chapter or section? I can think of four reasons.

1. That what you've just spent 50,000 words describing contains some major uncertainties or ambiguities requiring one last iteration. Just to ensure that you won't be taken out of context or have unintended meanings applied to your messages,

2. That the North, South, East, West elements you've just described require a conclusion along "this one is the best" lines — added for the sake of completeness,

3. That the landscape is about to change, with the conclusion preparing the reader for the volatility ahead (though such changes may need to have been discussed earlier),

4. That there's a major complementary body of work that can be included — partly as a refreshing twist in the narrative (a reward for making it this far) and partly as confirmatory evidence for your overall conclusions. That said, don't include it out of insecurity. Any "don't just take my word for it" style conclusion that acts as a crutch for your argument could do the opposite.

Accepted wisdom says that no new concepts should be added at this stage (add another chapter if you need to) although I've been guilty of doing exactly that for several of my books. The reason being that I thought the additional concept would act as the "icing on the cake" — perhaps offering a different way of looking at the same material but one that reinforced the overall message.

11. Jacket and cover copy

These are the words most likely to sell our project to potential readers. Additionally, the jacket copy often forms the basis for the press release (issued by your publisher). And it will be the blurb for *Amazon* and other bookselling websites. So — despite the thousands upon thousands of words already written — these might be the most important yet.

What's required are three or four pithy paras that make your writing project stand out from the crowd, assuming we've failed to win any glowingly positive review from *The Financial Times* or *Guardian* that can be used instead.

My best tip for this. Write the wildest most salesy, most aggressive "YOU'VE GOTTA READ THIS" 200-word description you can think of. Then edit it again, making it full of the wildest hyperbole imaginable. Then leave it for 24 hours and come back and see what cannot be substantiated.

Here, and here alone, a glass of wine or whatever it is you use to relax can help. It needs to flow better than poetry and have the rhythm of a Shakespeare sonnet. Here's the place for alliteration, *tricolons*, *epistrophes*, antitheses and every other trick you can think of. Just make it zing!

Still struggling? Perhaps start by asking a series of questions, though make them open questions.

"Have you ever wondered how Birmingham became the centre of the metal bashing industry?" could lead to the obvious riposte, and a lost potential reader, so try instead:

"How did a small group of industrialists turn an unfashionable Midlands town into the cradle of a global revolution?"

Broader, more intriguing, more enticing and a hint at the world your pages open.

We could then add some bullets. These can list what the reader will learn within, not in chapter order but overall. The big picture, with some intriguing details.

"You will discover:

- why Birmingham grew from a small town to become Britain's second city in a matter of decades,
- how the city sucked in industrialists, workers, bankers, speculators, criminals and vagabonds,
- the appalling conditions of the poor and the dark secrets and extravagance of the rich,
- the City's Edwardian patrons who created an astonishing global legacy."

Again, we've given nothing away except the promise of the treasures within.

Some other things to consider:

- The cover's no place to get technical. Instead state the promise of the book — what the reader will gain,
- Think about a strong headline and potentially add a killer standfirst (as described in Chapter Three). That and some bullets make a strong combination,
- Consider blending in a one- or two-line description of you, the author — starting the required justification process for why you are the person to be writing this work,
- And, yes, this is also the place for the best of the quotes from eminent peers or reviewers.

12. Biography

Two things about your biography. First, after the jacket blurb this is the key decider for browsers wondering about a purchase/download, so you need to make the case for why you're *the* person to write this book/white paper.

This goes beyond your qualifications and experience. That's just your claim to legitimacy. This is singling you out among your peers: your fixations, your unique insights, your offbeat experiences — all making you and you alone right for the task.

Second, it's another obvious chance to sell the book, so make sure you take it. Sure, tell them you went to Cambridge and what your PhD was on. Sure, tell them about your work in the Centre for Exactly What This Book's About. But also tell them about your decades-long mission to investigate this particular conundrum — and importantly why such a conundrum is possibly the most important thing they should be focused on right now.

Yes, the sell should be explicit or as near to explicit as we can make it without sounding like a used car salesman (unless that's the subject of the book, of course).

This from my second bestseller:

> "*Get Things Done* is the third of Robert's series of books looking into his personal history, and the psychology and early-life conditioning that created such an ineffective young adult."

So a hint at the series (as justification) and the unique insight within. And a couple of lines later I'm at it again…

> "While fear of failure [the subject of the first in the series] is an innate condition we must learn to accept and navigate, and confi-

dence [subject of the second] an alchemy we can create only once we learn to discriminate, Robert's view is that getting things done is little more than a process involving the generation of plans and adoption of habits based on our desires."

This is less biography and more sell, sell, sell (if you'll excuse the *epizeuxis*).

And, yes, write it in the third person, no matter how weird it feels. And no, this is not the place for a zany photo that reveals your wacky side. For anything professional, keep it corporate: a headshot with you wearing the uniform of your industry, whether that's Silicon Valley T-shirt-n-jeans or City of London Savile Row suit.

13. Footnotes, endnotes and references

Footnotes are certainly required for any peer-reviewed academic papers. It's also a strong habit for any work that seeks professional acceptance among peers to credit those peers when cited (to prevent accusations of plagiarism if nothing else) and certainly when quoted.

Yet my preference is that footnotes are in fact endnotes, which is a separate section at the back of the book or the end of each chapter or section. If at the end of the chapter or book they can even take on the form of "bonus material" — adding *bon mots* and anecdotes and other fluff.

Footnotes at the bottom of the page glare up distractingly, interrupting the reader journey we've spent so much time perfecting. Again, *Word* can help generate footnotes/endnotes and, yes, there's also an International Standard for citing references (ISO 690:2010 (en)), which you're welcome to make use of.

14. Killer titles

And with all that done, the process of actually producing page proofs for checking begins, after which we have — finally — a book that can be printed.

Except haven't we forgotten something? What about the book title? Sure, we may have had a working title but that was before we wrote the book. Some 50,000 words later we may feel differently. It could well be a very different book from the one we envisaged at the start. For instance, this book's working title was *How to Write Killer Non-fiction*, which quickly became inadequate.

Beyond the headline-writing tips in Chapter Four and the alliteration idea in Chapter Five, what else should we think about when settling on a final title?

Some thoughts on coming up with that killer title:

- Let's get back to the problem your writing project answers. What is that? As with headlines, write a generic sentence. And what's the solution within? Here, the problem was that so many people are asked or want to write long-form content and approach the project fearfully. And the solution within is that they can lose that fear through process, planning and step-by-step execution,
- And who are you writing for? Professionals in this case, but also amateur historians or chroniclers — anyone with that fabled "book in them". That's a wide audience, though not a deep one. This isn't a mass-consumer title, although non-fiction rarely is. There's a clear audience in mind, and it may be worth targeting them in the title,
- Don't be too clever. Those headline puns are great but often rely on distorting meanings to such as extent they lose resonance.

This needs to be the smack in the face — the sucker punch — though we can perhaps be more playful in the sub-title,

- And think about search-engine optimisation, especially for *Amazon* or *Google*. What would someone needing or wanting your book feed into that search box? The closer your title can get to that, the more often your work will come up in searches,

- Finally, make a list of all your rival titles, including their sub-headings. Somewhere within that list might be a combination of words that describe your work perfectly,

- It might also be worth thinking about what shouldn't be included. I quickly realised that the word *killer* was an unlikely SEO search term for those seeking help with their writing and that the term non-fiction was also off-putting: few people think "I really need to become a better *non-fiction* writer" when considering a writing project for work or pleasure.

What do they think about? In this case it was writing well, of course. I initially added *how* to after playing with the *Amazon* search engine to see what came up, although ultimately thought it unnecessary. Adding *work and pleasure* gave the book reach, all of which meant we now had the audience need, the promise and the range. A dab of alliteration and a final think about the inverted pyramid and I had it: *Writing Well for Work and Pleasure*, supported by a sub-heading that spelt out the offering further.

As we can see, like most things (and certainly most things in this book) it's more a process than an "a-ha" moment, though don't discount blinding flashes of inspiration. They do happen, though not always to you. The title of my best-selling book *What's Stopping You?* which some claim was a success precisely because of its title (demonstrating how important the right title can be) came to my wife as I explained my book-naming dilemma to her over breakfast. In fact, she had to say it twice because, the first time, I thought she was asking me a question and answered her literally.

And, yes, it is ironic that the last element written will be the first line read. But that sums up the process-driven writer's journey this book has been about from the start. I hope it's been helpful.

Appendix

Some books worth reading (or not) on English usage, style and writing

This is a "how to" book for professionals and hobbyists wanting to write long-form books, papers and articles. It's not a guide to English usage or style nor a general book about the craft of writing, although includes elements of both. That's because there's no gap in the market — plenty of books cover those genres.

There's nothing exhaustive about the choices below. It's a personal list of books I've found useful (or not) or enjoyable (ditto) over the years. There are many more, all pursuing slightly different audiences or angles. I've also divided the books roughly into those acting as reference or user guides, and those that — while full of tips — are written to be an enjoyable read.

I'm happy to hear recommendations but this is my pick

1.   Usage and style guides

The Economist Style Guide (first published 1986)

"On only two scores can *The Economist* hope to outdo its rivals consist-ently," *The Economist Style Guide* states in its introduction. "One is the quality of its analysis and the other is the quality of its writing."

In fact, the second of these maxims has proved more enduring than the first given the magazine's growing reputation for uncompro-mising cantankerousness to the point of arrogance. Meanwhile, it's rare to find fault with the quality of the writing.

The *Guide* encourages lucidity and clarity and discourages hec-toring, chattiness and, err, arrogance — a forgivable blindspot given that its key role is not as a *style* guide, as such, but as a guide to English usage for periodicals. *The Economist Style Guide* has settled countless arguments in my time as a journalist, sub-editor, editor, author and PR content provider, though it has also started a few. If in doubt, or if there's contradictory advice, *The Economist*'s view (at least on English usage) should take precedence.

Its A-Z format makes it a handy reference guide, even if the style is so engaging you'll want to read the next entry and the one after. And that brings me to its only real fault. The book was born from the need for the magazine's (or as it prefers to be known, the newspaper's) sub-editors to agree standard usage. And is therefore focused on *The Economist*'s core subjects, making it perfect for my work in the finance industry, though of more limited use in, say, health, food or the arts.

The Elements of Style, William Strunk Jr. and E.B. White (first pub-lished 1920)

A bit old and stuffy but still revered by purists as the first book of its type. Originally a course offered by Strunk (when professor of English at Cor-nell University), it was his student (and later author of *Charlotte's Web*)

E.B. White that turned Strunk's course notes into a publishing sensation.

The book has survived many updates and reprints to retain its original flavour — that of an authoritative lecturer giving his students a ticking off after too many bad essays. Indeed, modern sensibilities may object to the didactic tone, though the admonishments are worth noting nonetheless.

Despite the book's brevity (my version is just 96 pages) it packs a lot in: broadening from standard rules about the placing of commas and apostrophes to offer a reasonably complete ready-reckoner for good writing, including style. By Chapter Five it's telling writers to "place themselves in the background" (meaning that a focus on using language proficiently will allow your style to emerge, rather than the other way around); "write in a way that comes naturally" (rather than imitating others); and "work from a suitable design" (meaning first develop a strong structure) — all of which are perfect expressions of my thoughts in the preceding chapters.

While others, such as Zinsser (qv), have offered similar advice in a more digestible format and less coercive style, this is the original: hence remaining *the* reference book for many acclaimed writers.

Fowler's Dictionary of Modern English Usage, editor Jeremy Butterfield (first published 1926)

Still the daddy when it comes to the uses and abuses of the language. The jacket declares it "the world's most trusted reference book" and it's hard to argue otherwise. I mentioned earlier that the two indispensable tools of the trade are a thesaurus (the online version is fine) and a dictionary (which I prefer printed and well-thumbed). Yet, if permitted a third, *Fowler's* (also printed) would be it.

Another A-Z reference book and an unlikely one for a continuous read given its 928 pages, though it nonetheless manages to offer inarguable advice in an engaging style using real examples. It's entry on *nonetheless*, for instance, separated its use from *none the less* by quoting from the *Oxford Companion to Western Art, Dairy Field* magazine, G.K. Chesterton and the *Oxford Dictionary of National Biography*.

Churchill made all his officials read it (preceding Gowers (qv)), *The New York Times* declared *Fowler's* "sacred" and a "higher authority" while *The Spectator* called H.W. Fowler "a hero". In fact, it was originally the Fowler brothers. Henry Watson (born 1858) authored *Fowler's* alone, although the book remains dedicated to his younger brother Francis George Fowler (1871-1918) who died in 1918 of tuberculosis contracted while on active service in World War I, curtailing his career as a lexicographer alongside his brother.

Working in Guernsey as partners, the Fowler brothers produced the *King's English* (1906) and the *Concise Oxford English Dictionary* (1911). Their linguistic style was to avoid convolution, artificiality, archaic language or foreign phrases — making *Fowler's* a no-nonsense guide brought right up-to-date by editor Jeremy Butterfield.

Usage & Abusage, Eric Partridge (first published in 1942)

My copy — now battered and yellowing — was printed in 1981 and cost £2.25. It was my go-to reference for many years, eventually supplanted by the weightier *Fowler's*, although the two still compete furiously for my affections.

I love Partridge's waggish entries (such as "*ain't* for *isn't* or *is not* is an error so illiterate that I blush to record it") that were a gift to a frazzled sub-editor looking for sardonic ripostes when handed poor copy. But that's the problem with *Usage & Abusage*. Penguin's competitor to *Fowler's* (published by Oxford University Press) contains a little too much of Partridge's personality, making it an engaging but distracting read rather than the — as advertised — quick-flick handy-guide.

This feeling is reinforced by the alphabetical referencing being occasionally interrupted by essay-length entries such as the 4000-word thesis on Fused Particles (don't ask). Here, Partridge spends so much time referencing *Fowler's* that Penguin's handier offering clearly establishes itself on a lower rung in the hierarchy (explaining why I eventually traded up).

A New Zealander and Gallipoli veteran, Partridge was as interested in slang and colloquialisms as he was in correct English. He produced *A Dictionary of Slang and Unconventional English* in 1937 and the intriguingly titled *A Dictionary of the Underworld* in 1950. He was also a prolific novelist, publishing under the *nom de plume* Corrie Denison.

The King's English, Kingsley Amis (1997)

Amis attempts the same trick as Partridge and *The Economist* — an A-Z formatted reference guide that nonetheless makes a great read — though he wins only a four-star rather than five-star review for his troubles. Sure, there's something hypnotic about both the structure of the book and Amis's writing, and it's probably the only one likely to make you laugh out loud. But then that's Amis's clear intention.

Published as recently as 1997, it still reads as if from a previous era: a pre-internet age in which his grumblings about vocabulary becoming Americanised now seem quaint. That said, his opinions on the usage and abusage of English are sound, even if his illustrations feel increasingly unsound. For instance, he explains the application of commas in lists with the phrase "Samantha is twenty years old, blue-eyed and has a large bust". He claims the correct version replaces the comma with a further "and" as the phrase contained two lists rather than one — not that you're still paying attention.

Rather like Stephen King (qv) — who could have adopted the same pun in the title, though the original *King's English* was written by the Fowler brothers (as cited above) — this is a celebrity writer being self-indulgent after a successful writing career. That said, Amis manages to keep the rambling anecdotes to a minimum, even if — at times —

it does read like someone chastising their dinner guests after downing a very agreeable bottle of claret.

Butcher's Copy-editing, editors Judith Butcher, Caroline Drake and Maureen Leach (first published in 1975 with Judith Butcher the original editor)

A comprehensive copy-editor's reference manual published by Cambridge University Press. This is specialist information for the publishing industry and comes at a specialist price (my copy cost £45 in 2008).

Butcher's takes authors through the publishing process — from copy-editing to page-proofs to camera-ready copy (also called "bromides" or "Ozalids") — while explaining the jargon, proof markings and standards of the industry: everything from abbreviations to zoological names. The glossary alone runs to 21 pages and the index to 33, such is the breadth and depth of coverage. There are sections on science and mathematics books, law books, and even on publishing music. If you want to use phonetics, Old English, Russian, Hebrew, Arabic or Chinese, you're covered.

Butcher's gets under the bonnet of the publishing world to examine the industry's nuts and bolts as well as its *rectos* and *versos*. It's publishing's equivalent of a *Haynes Manual* (those famous car-maintenance workshop guides that no doubt rely on *Butcher's* when being edited).

The Oxford Dictionary of English Grammar, editors Sylvia Chalker and Edmund Weiner (first published 1983)

Since 2014, there's been a second edition (including Bas Aarts as an editor), though it's my own edition — acquired around 1990 and covered in coffee-stains — that I opine on here.

Bought in a panic having landed a job as a sub-editor on a financial magazine and without the requisite expensive education likely to see me confidently through the task (of editing everyone else's copy), this was my crutch. Except it wasn't. The coffee stains attest to the fact it found more use as a coaster than a must-have reference guide.

I'm not sure why. Other guides seemed more digestible, somehow more on the money. Easier to use. And it seemed to lack what I really needed, which was a definitive reference preventing me falling foul of archaic grammar rules, which were always described well enough though often failed to solve my immediate dilemma.

Ultimately, it just never seemed to provide the answer — or it did but not in a form I could grab on the fly and apply immediately. This probably says more about my short attention span than the book's failings, of course, though I eventually supplemented this larger tome with the *Oxford Pocket English Grammar* (1990), edited by A.J. Thomson and A.V. Martinet, which seemed easier to use. It had an index and a table of contents and was divided into broad areas of concern such as spelling rules and tenses — all of which meant I found the nub of my problem more quickly, as well as the answer.

The Complete Plain Words, Sir Ernest Gowers (1954)

In *Politics and the English Language* (1946) (qv) George Orwell rails against the decadence of post-war British civilisation, using the abuse of the English language as Exhibit A. It had grown ugly and inaccurate, he opined, and thought the cure was a return to preferring Anglo-Saxon over Latin/French derived words.

He'd have found an unlikely ally in Sir Ernest Gowers, a former President of the English Association. Both saw the problem lying deep within the bowels of British government: the civil service, whose power had grown exponentially during in the war years. Far from delivering the promised "sunlit uplands" of the post-war era, civil servants were presiding over a stultifying bureaucracy wrapped in impenetrable officialese.

Gowers, who'd previously written *Plain Words* (1948) and the *ABC of Plain Words* (1951), was tasked by HM Treasury to find a cure, the result of which was *The Complete Plain Words* published in 1954. "I suspect that this project may be received by many of them without any marked enthusiasm or gratitude," Gowers confesses in the prologue, the "them" being civil servants addicted to pomposity, obfuscation and long-winded diffuse verbiage in their written communications.

"The official must be the interpreter," was Gowers' view — aiding wider understanding rather than using language as an exercise in gatekeeping. And, like Orwell, he thought this mainly down to the simple point of choosing unambiguous language.

After giving the reader a stern talking-to, the book relaxes a little to offer writers guidance on the choice of words divided into various buckets such as "avoiding superfluous words" "choosing familiar words" and "choosing precise words". And there's sections on grammar, syntax and punctuation.

2.   Books on writing

On Writing Well, William Zinsser (first published 1976)

By far my favourite writing guide and a book our PR firm gifts to all new employees, though not all of them read it. I know this because I can tell from their writing. Those that have read it improve quickly and gain confidence as they improve. Those that don't — usually because they think they don't need to — become defensive when their work is rewritten, and slowly lose confidence.

Zinsser's classic work is highly readable with anecdotes and war stories aplenty while never losing the narrative's thread. For instance, in Chapter Two of this book, I claim that good writing takes time and effort. That it's hard work. Zinsser agrees by relating an encounter with a writer claiming the opposite — that writing's easy, fun, and that it should come easily or not at all. If the mood doesn't take you, "go fishing," he said, while Zinsser insists we battle on.

He's right of course, as he is on so many things. Occasionally, he lapses into hectoring, such as his early diatribe on adjectives, though (unlike Gowers or Strunk) he never moralises. Mostly, this is a great writer passing on his craft in sympathetic tones — and I was glad to see a thirtieth anniversary reprint, which meant I no-longer had to search *Amazon* or *eBay* for used editions from American sellers that took weeks to ship.

Zinsser died in 2015 after a career in journalism, literary criticism, editing and teaching (at Yale and Columbia universities). He also wrote 18 books and defined success as "doing what you want to do and doing it well" (though he never said it should be easy, note). Over the years, I've bought close to 100 copies of *On Writing Well* for my staff, and I'm indebted to him for making my life as a writer, editor, sub-editor and manager easier.

Why I Write, George Orwell (first published 1946)

The title of a 1946 essay, though now a Penguin volume that includes *A Hanging* (first published 1931), *The Lion & the Unicorn* (1940) and *Politics and the English Language* (1946). All are essays showing Orwell's writing at his finest, even if they involve subjects not relevant to the craft. Indeed, *The Hanging*, which describes an execution in Burma, is a masterclass in taut, intense and evocative reportage.

In *Why I Write* he claims four great motives for writing.

1. Sheer egoism: a desire to seem clever and to be remembered after death,
2. Aesthetic enthusiasm: a desire to share experiences and your perception of beauty,

3. Historical impulse: a need to find facts and present them,

4. Political purpose: the desire to push the world in a certain direction.

He uses the word *political* in the widest possible sense, allowing us to include professional writing within his purview.

And in *Politics and the English Language*, Orwell sets out six rules for writing, all of which still make sense three-quarters of a century later.

1. Never use a metaphor, simile or other figure of speech which you are used to seeing in print,

2. Never use a long word where a short one will do,

3. If it is possible to cut a word out, always cut it out,

4. Never use the passive where you can use the active,

5. Never use a foreign phrase, scientific word or a jargon word if you can think of an everyday English equivalent,

6. Break any of these rules sooner than say anything outright barbarous.

On Writing, Stephen King (2000)

King calls this book a "Memoir of the Craft", which is the best thing about the entire book: correctly labelling writing as a craft. But it was page 125 of my edition before he said anything of use, which I'd be fine with if it wasn't for the reviews on the back. "Absolutely fascinating…basic in-structions…sensible advice," said the *The Sunday Times* — apparently.

Admittedly, after page 125 he settles into his instructive role, with the anecdotes and reminiscences giving way to a highly readable digest of his trade. Here, his writing skills shine through, with advice delivered like an elder passing on wisdom to a protégé, which makes a refreshing change from the "and another thing" ramblings of Amis *et al.*

Yet there's an additional problem. His trade is fiction. He deals with scene-setting, suspense and dialogue brilliantly. For structuring complex arguments and making technicalities compelling, this book is less useful. Many of his aphorisms are also somewhat obvious: "The road to hell is paved with adverbs". "To write is human, to edit is divine". "Description begins in the writer's imagination but should finish in the reader's". There's more — though they eventually grate.

Waterhouse on Newspaper Style, Keith Waterhouse, (first published 1989)

From novelists to tabloid hacks, and a book that Orwell, Gowers or even Amis and King would have treated as a treatise on the corruption of English. But it's equally redolent of its time and place — and highly loveable. Like a roguish poacher divulging his craft, Waterhouse explains the tabloids' trade in terms of words-on-the-page rather than *paparazzi* stakeouts and shouted letterbox bribes.

Through hundreds of examples — good and bad — the skill of Britain's popular press is exposed in all its "shock horror" detail. Here's why *The Sun* famously had the best paid subs in Fleet Street: their ability to use the English language to entice, tease, enrage and amuse (as well as inform and educate, of course!).

Yet Waterhouse, a Yorkshireman, was no fan of hackery. The book started life as the *Daily Mirror* style guide, intended to raise what he saw as slipping standards among the journalists. And he followed it up with *English Our English (And How To Sing It)* (1994) that railed against — not the decline of English usage — but its poor teaching in schools and in the home.

Although a prolific writer — the author of *Billy Liar* and the West End play *Jeffrey Bernard is Unwell*, as well as the *Low Life* column in *The Spectator* — Waterhouse's first love remained newspapers. He died in 2009 before the 2011-12 *Leveson Inquiry* pulled the tabloids' teeth and just as search-engine optimisation was destroying the subtleties of the newspaper journalist's art: making *Waterhouse on Newspaper Style* a collector's item, though one worth reading nonetheless.

Eats Shoots & Leaves, Lynne Truss (2003)

Keith Waterhouse founded the *Association for the Abolition of the Aberrant Apostrophe.* I've no idea whether Lynne Truss was a member, though they'd have approved of each other's prejudices against poor punctuation.

Eats Shoots & Leaves is that rare thing: a bestselling book on punctuation. Perhaps it was clever marketing by Profile Books or that genius title. Certainly, the book itself — usually sold as a small hardback — is pleasing to the eye and feels nice to hold. But mainly it's the author's wit in dissecting a subject that many people struggle with that makes this such a "crossover" book — though she'd warmed up her audience with a well-received Radio 4 series called *Cutting a Dash.*

Yet there's something about this book that irritates. It's just a tad too clever. Even a little smug. It's also somewhat twee — spending too much time off-topic, like an aging celebrity assuming a receptive audience while throwing out anecdotes.

If you're one of those types that has Radio 4 on in the house all day and worries about the encroachment of your neighbour's hedge, my guess is you'll like this book. It has that Earl Grey tea and Victoria sponge suburban feel to it. But if you want a book that informs or settles disputes, then this isn't it. There's no index, the table of contents is too brief and the chapter headings too broad to be useful.

That said, the fact it entertains more than informs shouldn't condemn it, not least because Truss would no doubt claim that it isn't trying to be a user-guide or manual. Though the fact its billing suggests otherwise can leave the reader dissatisfied, which is why it belongs more among the writing books than the user guides.

The Elements of Eloquence, Mark Forsyth (2013)

If Lynne Truss's obsession is punctuation, Mark Forsyth's is the English phrase. His two previous works — *The Etymologicon* and *The Horolog-*

icon — tour the English language's hidden recesses for (respectively) unexpected connections and lost speech. Here, he tackles the making of "the perfect English phrase".

Beautifully and eloquently written, as you'd expect, the book is a constant delight — so much so that it shouldn't be read in a hurry nor be used as a reference guide.

The book opens brilliantly with a Preface that starts:

"Shakespeare was not a genius. He was, without the distant shadow of a doubt, the most wonderful writer who ever breathed. But not a genius."

Instead, according to Forsyth, the Bard learnt tricks. Techniques that become more prevalent as his writing progressed — explaining why his later plays (*King Lear*, *Macbeth* etc.) are more quoted than his earlier ones (*The Two Gentlemen of Verona*, *Titus Andronicus* etc.).

And then we learn the tricks, some of which I've referenced (with due credit to Forsyth) in Chapter Five. Each is enchanting. A treat. It's like opening a door into an unseen world of illusion and wizardry, in which we graduate into the magic circle from being muggles. Even the names have a touch of magic about them: whether a *polyptoton*, a *merism*, a *synaesthesia*, an *aposiopesis* or a *hyperbaton* (there are many more). Each is an offputtingly complex word for something lovely, that enlivens writing and makes it memorable.

A product of Winchester School and Lincoln College Oxford, Forsyth has certainly not wasted his educational privileges, instead gifting us a series of books — as well as the wonderful *Inky Fool* blog — that will make you fall head over heels in love with the English language. And if your love was already confirmed, Forsyth will make you obsessed.

Rarely is such a delightful read so full of insight.

Everybody Writes, Ann Handley (2014)

Potentially an American version of this book in that it focuses on the wider process of content generation — calling itself a "go-to guide to creating ridiculously good content". I also rarely disagree with Handley's tips and recommendations: she knows her craft.

But I have two criticisms. First, it's very bitty, as if pandering to these attention deficit times by offering tight vignettes for easy digestion. Some are barely 200 words while others stretch to a couple of pages, never more. There are 74 of them, 84 if counting her *Content Tools*. And, yes, they certainly add up to something reasonably comprehensive. But the format feels like a compromise between the short entries of the user guides and the longer narrative of the style books — a half-way house that doesn't quite work because you (or at least I) become reluctant to absorb so much disparate information so quickly.

Second, despite being rammed with useful tips it never quite grips the reader. It's too light. Too chatty. And suffers a tad from the breezy style that Zinsser and Strunk warn against. It's one of those books that tries so hard to be your friend that it ends up becoming irritating. Partly, I put this down to Handley trying to encompass short-form internet writing — including sections on writing for *LinkedIn* (and even writing your *LinkedIn* profile). And partly it's just Handley's style: one that occasionally sacrifices focus for amiability.

First You Write a Sentence, Joe Moran (2018)

A novel idea but an obvious one. If a songwriter thinks in melodies and an artist in shapes and colours then a writer thinks in sentences, or should do. They're the widgets of our craft, says Moran. They have nouns and verbs and conjunctions and prepositions placed in an order that gives them meaning and grace. And they make sense of the world.

Sentences are the verbal constellations that define us, which makes them so powerful that it's worth learning how to write them well, insists Moran. They need precision, rhythm and a human rather than mechanical syntax. All of which Moran — a professor of English and Cultural History at Liverpool John Moores University — delivers in this elegant gem of a book.

Is there a "but" coming? There is. Moran is somewhat trapped by his premise, meaning that every sentence feels like it's trying too hard. It gets tiring after a while. And then there's the fact he falls into purple prose (i.e. being overly florid) too often to be entirely forgivable. Try this on rhythm:

"Rhythm is the song of life. The syllabic stress patterns of speech sync up with the heartbeat we hear in the womb, the pulses of air in the lungs, the strides of walking and running..."

I'll spare you the rest.

Sure, some will love it — but it makes the book more a love-letter to a particular (though important) element of writing rather than a style guide for shaping the perfect sentence (though there's plenty of learning within). Still a lovely book though.

The Sense of Style, Steven Pinker (2014)

As a cognitive psychologist and popular scientist, Steven Pinker has his detractors though I love his optimistic take on humanity. And as a writer writing on the English language, he's managed something remarkable: a book that marries the unregulated chaos of English — in our age of digital publishing and technocratic authority — with the need for strong prose and good grammar.

Pinker's famed faith in humanity shines through, allowing the reader to absorb knowledge without having to endure the disparaging lectures and admonishments of older books in the genre. Indeed, while saying he loved Strunk and White (qv) he avoids their didactic tone — instead seeing English usage as a science. One that simply needs explaining well.

Yet the book has several faults. First, it's peppered with cartoons (no Dilberts, but close) and the odd pseudo-scientific chart explaining sentence structures or syntax obscurities or something else that doesn't require a graph to explain it. The inclusion of both in fact reveals the book's ambiguity. Is this a hardcore instruction manual for teaching English usage? It certainly wants to be. Or is this an engaging Zinsser-style easy-read for English language buffs? It wants to be that too, though at times his convoluted take can make for heavy reading — hence the use of cartoons to inject levity into what's occasionally a dense read.

And that's the second fault. This is a scientist writing about a craft. Exactness matters — not to aid understanding or ease the reader's journey but for its own sake. He even picks on Strunk and White for their "botched" examples and "tenuous grasp of grammar" and Orwell for using the passive voice when deriding the use of the passive voice in *Politics and the English Language* (qv). All of which leaves me thinking that Pinker's goal is to tame and order a language that cannot be tamed and doesn't require the OCD-level order he prescribes.

Yet he just as frequently pulls himself up for his pedantry, allowing us mere mortals the bandwidth to include forgivable errors for the sake of clarity or "grace". And his writing never fully loses its humanity or enthusiasm — making the book feel like the work of an eccentric scientist conducting experiments that leave him with a blackened face and singed hair, and with his students looking on with a mix of admiration, incredulity and fear (to end fittingly on a *tricolon*).

Index